Shakespeare's
Julius Caesar:
A Critical Introduction

Cedric Watts

PublishNation

ISBN: 978-1-326-40237-2

PublishNation, London.

Contents

Chapter 1: Preliminaries

Characteristics of *Julius Caesar*

Shakespeare's *Julius Caesar* is so potent a play about history that it has helped to make history: it has inspired not only the assassin of an American President but also a convict who became a revered statesman.

Julius Caesar is the first tragedy of Shakespeare's great mature phase. His previous tragedies, *Titus Andronicus* and *Romeo and Juliet*, both had strikingly original features, the former being a nightmarishly vivid revenge drama, the latter being a brilliant tragedy of young love. In *Julius Caesar*, however, we encounter a masterly political drama, in which Shakespeare meets the challenge of dealing with one of the most famous events in classical history, the assassination of the great Caesar. "It was a new kind of political play", says David Daniell, "combining fast action (it is a short play – just over half the length of *Hamlet*) and compelling rhetoric." Muriel Bradbrook termed it "the first modern political drama of the English stage". With confidence and panache, Shakespeare dramatises the events leading up to the assassination: in particular, the conspirators' crafty endeavour to enlist the noble Brutus in their ranks. The assassination follows, a central eruption of violence; and thereafter events unfold with intensely ironic logic. There's no sub-plot, just one main plot;

and it hinges on two questions: 1: Will Caesar be assassinated?; and 2: Will the assassins get away with it?

Shakespeare thus returns to the political theme he had recently orchestrated in his second tetralogy of history plays (*Richard II, Henry IV, Parts 1 and 2,* and *Henry V*): namely, that rebellion against a leader may unleash civil war and bring woe upon the rebels. Once again he explores conflicts between honour, patriotism and expediency, and between private and public loyalties.

Julius Caesar is so replete with famous incidents and speeches that, even if we are reading it or seeing it for the first time, we may well have that *déjà-vu* feeling: the drama may seem to be quoting itself. The murder of Caesar; the memorable rhetoric: "Beware the Ides of March'"; "Why, man, he doth bestride the narrow world / Like a Colossus"; "The fault, dear Brutus, is not in our stars, / But in ourselves, that we are underlings"; "*Et tu, Brute?*"; "Friends, Romans, countrymen: lend me your ears"; "There is a tide in the affairs of men / Which, taken at the flood, leads on to fortune": again and again the work shimmers with the aura of its own fame and seems to echo its own resonant oratory, reminding us proudly of itself. Here Shakespeare is on top form as a master of the quotable epitome, offering (in Alexander Pope's words) "What oft was thought, but ne'er so well expressed". And those literary epitomes demonstrably influence real lives.

Another paradoxical feature of the play is this: as it ages, it seems the more authoritatively topical. That is to say, since its first performance in 1599, the passing centuries have provided more and more historical evidence to verify its shrewd insights into political chicanery, hypocrisy, cruelty and folly. We may recall George Bernard Shaw's observation:

In truth, the period of time covered by history is far too short to allow of any perceptible progress in the...Evolution of the Human Species. The notion that there has been any such progress since Caesar's time...is too absurd for discussion.

The assassins of Caesar set a precedent for the numerous political assassinations which have marked history; and the bomb-plotters' attempt to kill Adolf Hitler in 1944 is a stark reminder that attempted assassination can still, sometimes, appear laudable.

Julius Caesar is also one of Shakespeare's most controversial plays. Ernest Schanzer says:

Commentators have been quite unable to agree on who is its principal character or whether it has one; on whether it is a tragedy and, if so, of what kind; on whether Shakespeare wants us to consider the assassination damnable or praiseworthy; while of all the chief characters of the play contradictory interpretations have been given.

The play is, in large measure, an experiment in realism, characterised by the fact that every one of the main characters is flawed; and, repeatedly, an action which promises to be conclusive serves only to provoke a reaction. And, though it is satisfactorily conclusive, *Julius Caesar* is open-ended, too, for the story of the relationship between Octavius and Mark Antony will not be completed until the end of *Antony and Cleopatra.*

The real Emperor Augustus (Octavius) is reported to have said, when dying: "Have I played the part well? Then applaud as I exit." Exploiting theatricality, *Julius Caesar* depicts politics as theatre. Politicians are actors; Romans seek to live the parts they play, to become their roles, and to transcend the private selves, the performers behind the performance. Yet, with recurrent irony, the fallible physical self mocks the persona, the "mask" worn by the public self, while the private life reveals a more sympathetic individual. Seeking to transcend the temporal, aiming for supreme power or historic immortality, these leading actors achieve, ironically, the shortening of their life-spans. But, historically, Caesar's name would survive; the month of July commemorates him; and his family name (cognomen) became a title meaning "Emperor" in such usages as "Tsar" (or "Czar") and "Kaiser". His heir is commemorated by the month of August.

The political questions that *Julius Caesar* raises endure to this day. Is political assassination ever justified? Does a good intention justify a bad means, or does the bad means mar the outcome? Does political commitment reduce human empathy? Are politicians' plans doomed to be mocked by unfolding events? Must violence always breed violence?

"The pen is mightier than the sword", wrote Edward Bulwer-Lytton in 1839. Shakespeare's quill-pen, writing *Julius Caesar*, has caused weapons to be used; this play, in which assassins smear themselves with gore, has drawn real blood.

What was the play's historical basis?

Repeatedly, the following factual list augments the play's ironies: see, for example, how Caesar treated such enemies as Brutus and Cassius. It also shows how Shakespeare has compressed the historical time-scale between March of 44 B.C. and October of 42 B.C. (Incidentally, I use the traditional term, "B.C.", i.e. "Before Christ", and eschew the politically-incorrect term "B.C.E", meaning "Before the [non-existent] Common Era".)

509 B.C.: The era of Roman monarchies ends; the Roman republic is established. In the republic, citizens of Rome meet at an annual assembly to elect their officials, the highest being two consuls, others being judges, magistrates and tax-collectors. There are also ten "Tribunes of the People" to represent the poor. The consuls are advised by a Senate of about 600 leading men, mostly rich noblemen, whose decisions tend naturally to favour themselves. Women and slaves have no vote.

106 B.C:. Pompey ("the Great") born.

Circa [around]100 B.C.: Gaius Julius Caesar born. His clan, called "Julia", claimed descent from Aeneas, the exiled Trojan prince, who was said to be the son of the goddess Venus. His cognomen "Caesar" has various possible origins. One notion is that an ancestor was born by caesarean section (from the Latin verb *caedere, caesum*, to cut). Another is that in battle an ancestor slew an elephant, "which in the Moorish tongue is called *caesai*", says the

Historia Augusta; and, when in power, Caesar would issue coins bearing the image of an elephant.

3 October, *c.* 87 B.C.: Gaius Cassius Longinus (Cassius) born.

June, 85 B.C.: Marcus Junius Brutus the Younger (Brutus) born.

14 January, 83 B.C.: Marcus Antonius (Mark Antony) born.

23 September, 63 B.C.: Gaius Octavius born.

59 B.C.: the First Triumvirate formed: Caesar, Pompey and Crassus rule Rome. Pompey marries Caesar's daughter, Julia. Caesar marries Calpurnia ("Calphurnia" in Shakespeare's play).

49 B.C.: After successful campaigns against the Gauls, Julius Caesar, now the leading general of the Roman Republic, crosses the river Rubicon with an army, defying the Roman Senate's order to lay down his arms. Civil war ensues. (Republican Rome had long been crumbling, as powerful dynasts such as Sulla, Crassus and Pompey ignored the Senate and became autocratic, backed by their own troops.)

48 B.C.: In the civil war, Caesar defeats Pompey at the Battle of Pharsalus. Pompey is later murdered by the Egyptian Pharaoh. Brutus, who had fought for Pompey, apologises to Caesar, who forgives him, making him Governor of Egypt in 46 B.C. and a praetor (magistrate) in 45 B.C.. Cassius, too, had fought for Pompey; yet, after surrendering, he was made a legate by Caesar.

45 B.C.: At the battle of Munda, Caesar defeats two sons of Pompey.

Brutus divorces his first wife and marries Porcia Catonis (Portia), daughter of a republican foe of Caesar, Cato the Younger. (Cassius was married to

Brutus's half-sister, and thus was Brutus's brother-in-law.)

44 B.C.: In February, Caesar is declared "dictator in perpetuity". Though popular with the lower classes, for whom he has provided feasts and shows, Caesar is opposed by many patricians, members of the nobility.

On the Ides (15th) of March, Caesar is assassinated by a crowd of patricians led by Brutus. The lower classes turn against the assassins. Civil war ensues: Brutus and his ally Cassius are opposed by the forces of Mark Antony, Gaius Octavius (aged 18) and Marcus Aemilius Lepidus, who form a new triumvirate, a ruling trio. (The name of Octavius, Caesar's great-nephew and adopted heir, formally becomes "Gaius Julius Caesar Octavianus".)

42 B.C.: The Senate declares Julius Caesar a god. At the Battle of Philippi, initially Cassius is defeated by Antony, but Brutus defeats Octavius; and, in the second phase of the battle, Brutus in turn is defeated. On 3 October, Cassius is slain at his own request by one of his men; and, on 23 October, Brutus commits suicide.

40 B.C.: Octavius defeats rebels. Mark Antony, lover of the Egyptian Queen, Cleopatra, marries Octavius's sister, Octavia Minor.

36 B.C.: Lepidus is forced into exile by Octavius.

31 B.C.: Civil war between Octavius and Mark Antony. At the Battle of Actium in September, the forces of Antony and Cleopatra are defeated. Antony and Cleopatra flee to Alexandria.

1 August, 30 B.C.: Mark Antony commits suicide. Later, so does Cleopatra. Octavius decrees the death of Caesarion, son of Cleopatra and Julius Caesar.

27 B.C.: The Senate confers upon Octavius the titles "Augustus" and "Princeps": "Illustrious" and "Chief". Octavius will term himself "Imperator Caesar divi filius": "Commander-Emperor Caesar, son of the god". Thus Octavius becomes Emperor, and, though republican forms are nominally retained, the republic is in practice superseded. During his long reign, the Roman empire enjoys relative peace and prosperity; the *Pax Romana* (era of Roman peace) is established; and the arts flourish. Poets, architects and sculptors hail a new Golden Age. The poet Horace, who had served in Brutus's army, is befriended by Octavius, who is said to have commissioned Virgil's *Aeneid*.

19 August, A.D. 14: Octavius dies (possibly poisoned by his wife Livia).

Julius Caesar: a summary of the plot

(The summary exposes ironic patterns, large and small, which are an important feature of *Julius Caesar*.)

Before the play:
At the Battle of Pharsalus, Caesar has defeated Pompey the Great in a civil war. In Egypt, Pompey is then murdered. Cleopatra, ousted by her brother, is reinstated by Caesar and becomes sole ruler of Egypt. Cleopatra gives birth to a son, Caesarion, fathered by Caesar.

Act 1:
(Sc. 1) In Rome, commoners celebrating Caesar's triumph are rebuked by two tribunes, because Caesar had defeated not a foreigner but the great Roman general, Pompey. The tribunes fear the growth of Caesar's power. (Later they are both "put to silence".)

(Sc. 2) Caesar is warned by a soothsayer to beware the Ides of March, March 15th. (The "ides", or, in Latin, *"idus"*, named a day near the middle of a month: in most months, the 13th; in March, May, July and October, the 15th. The date was originally determined by the first full moon of the year. Though plural in form, the phrase has singular application to one particular day.) Cassius seeks to persuade Brutus that Caesar "is now become a god" and needs to be dealt with. Brutus expresses sympathy with Cassius's views. Caska reports that Caesar was offered a crown but reluctantly declined it; later Caesar fell down and foamed at the mouth.

14

(Sc. 3) Caska reports fearsome supernatural events to Cicero. Cassius stirs Caska against Caesar. Cinna and Caska stress the importance of enlisting the highly-regarded Brutus in the conspirators' cause, to make it seem worthy.

Act 2:

(Sc. 1) Brutus reflects that since Caesar, at present, is blameless ("the quarrel will bear no colour for the thing he is"), the justification for assassinating him must be based on predictions that in the future Caesar would become tyrannical. A letter urges Brutus to emulate his ancestor, the Brutus (Lucius Junius Brutus) who had cast Tarquin out of Rome "when he was called king". The conspirators visit Brutus, who agrees to join them. Cassius wants them to kill Mark Antony too, but Brutus refuses to permit this. After the conspirators have left, Portia, Brutus's wife, reproaches him for being aloof and preoccupied; he promises to reveal the cause to her. Ligarius enters and says that he will join any venture if Brutus ("Soul of Rome") leads him.

(Sc. 2) Calphurnia, Caesar's wife, reports dire supernatural events, and tells Caesar that they show he should not venture forth to the Senate House. A servant states that the augurers, too, tell Caesar to stay at home. Caesar is persuaded to stay. Then Decius, a conspirator, enters and says that the Senators plan to give Caesar a crown and would comment "Lo, Caesar is afraid" if he were not to appear. Caesar changes his mind and, accompanied by conspirators, sets out.

15

(Scenes 3 and 4) Both Artemidorus and a soothsayer (i.e., a "truth-teller" or mystical forecaster) wish to warn Caesar of danger.

Act 3:

(Sc. 1) In the Senate House, Metellus and others ask Caesar to repeal the banishment of Metellus's brother. Caesar, declaring "I am constant as the Northern Star", refuses the request. The conspirators then stab Caesar to death and smear themselves with his blood. Brutus (in spite of Cassius's warnings) agrees to let Mark Antony give a subsequent funeral oration. When alone, Antony reveals his deep loyalty to Caesar and prophesies that "Domestic fury and fierce civil strife / Shall cumber all the parts of Italy."

(Sc. 2) At the Forum, Brutus addresses the people, explaining that Caesar was slain for being ambitious. The people approve him. Then Mark Antony speaks. Though he says he is "no orator, as Brutus is", he gradually arouses the populace to anger against the assassins. He reveals that Caesar's will bequeaths money and land to the people. Antony's hearers, incensed, set out to burn down the conspirators' houses. Brutus and Cassius flee; Octavius arrives to help Mark Antony.

(Sc. 2) The mob murders the innocent Cinna, a poet, having initially mistaken him for Cinna the conspirator.

Act 4:

(Sc. 1) Antony, Octavius and Lepidus (the Triumvirate) decide who should be sentenced to death. Lepidus is sent to fetch Caesar's will, so that it can be used to finance the Triumvirate. Antony says

16

that when Lepidus has served his purpose he should be cast off.

(Sc. 2) Brutus and Cassius quarrel bitterly (Brutus accusing Cassius of greed and corruption) but eventually are reconciled. Brutus has been told of the suicide of his wife. Later, Caesar's ghost appears to Brutus, saying "Thou shalt see me at Philippi" (and Brutus will indeed see him there).

Act 5:

(Sc. 1) At Philippi, on the eve of battle, the leaders of the opposed factions defy each other. Cassius (troubled by adverse omens) and Brutus say mutual farewells.

(Sc.3) Cassius, defeated by Mark Antony, wrongly thinks that his man Titinius has been captured and that the enemy has prevailed. Accordingly, Cassius dies, having instructed his servant Pindarus to stab him. Titinius enters, explaining that though Antony has defeated Cassius's forces, Brutus has prevailed against Octavius.

(Sc. 5) Now facing defeat, Brutus (with the aid of Strato) kills himself. The victors, Antony and Octavius, look on his body, and Antony declares "This was the noblest Roman of them all".

A note on the text and conventions used here

Julius Caesar was originally published in the First Folio (1623), the first collected edition of Shakespeare's works. I naturally use the accessible text of *Julius Caesar* edited by Cedric Watts (Ware: Wordsworth Editions, 2004), which faithfully retains the First Folio's spellings of certain names: "Caska" and "Calphurnia", for instance, where other editions have "Casca" and "Calpurnia". With the sole exception of an acknowledged quotation from the Peter Alexander edition, all quotations from *Julius Caesar* are from the Watts edition.

When we read a play by Shakespeare, the characters are products of the words on the page and the reader's imagination. Such characters may be based on real people, but they are artificial constructs, products of art. Nevertheless, in this study, I shall frequently talk of the characters as if they were real people with distinctive natures. This is not a sign of naive credulity. When we are dealing with a largely realistic text, it happens to be the most concise, comprehensive and lucid way of discussing the features that these constructs present to the imagination. As Dr Johnson remarked:

Imitations produce pain or pleasure, not because they are mistaken for realities, but because they being realities to mind.

Accordingly, in discussions of characters, I employ what A. D. Nuttall, in *A New Mimesis*, terms "transparent language". Having a democratic bias, I try to avoid the use of intimidating jargon.

In addition, though I place the characters in various historical contexts, my approach eschews the term "historicist". In *The Open Society and Its Enemies* and *The Poverty of Historicism*, the philosopher Karl Popper influentially defined "historicism" as the imposition of a false pattern on history. But I note readings deriving from "New Historicism", as it is called, alongside feminist, left-wing and (what may be loosely termed) liberal humanist readings.

How does Shakespeare alter the source-materials?

The funeral oration by Mark Antony may derive some features from Appian's *The Civil Wars*; but Shakespeare's main source for the play was Sir Thomas North's translation of Plutarch's *Lives of the Noble Grecians and Romanes*, 1579. Plutarch wrote in Greek; North translated into English the French translation by Jacques Amyot of the original Greek text. Plutarch took a complex view of Caesar. He notes Caesar's great achievements in war, his eloquence, and his ability to win popularity. He also notes that Caesar could be unscrupulous and desired to be called king; nevertheless, he imposed order, and his killers were punished by the gods.

Shakespeare "transformed a confused welter of historical fact and legend into taut, balanced, and supremely ambivalent drama", says Robert S. Miola. In the interests of dramatic pace and clarity, Shakespeare omits much of Plutarch's account. Plutarch gives lengthy descriptions of Caesar's military campaigns (in which Caesar proved to be a brilliant, brave and sometimes ruthless general), and he tells how Caesar sought to rebuild the destroyed cities of Carthage and Corinth, planned to drain marshes and construct harbours, and even reformed the calendar. Such matters are largely ignored by Shakespeare. But Shakespeare also suppressed material incriminating Caesar (who could be cruel and who was an inveterate womaniser), and says nothing of past enmity between Caesar and the

Senate. As in Plutarch, the Senate depicted by Shakespeare seeks to offer Caesar the crown (1.3.85-8, 22.93-4).

If you look again at our "Historical Chronology", you'll see that the play also compresses drastically the time-scale. For instance, historically, Caesar's triumph, or celebration, cited in Act 1, scene 1, had taken place in October; the Lupercalia (the fertility festival of Act 1, scene 2) took place subsequently in February, between the 13th and 15th, usually on the 15th; the assassination was committed on March 15; Caesar's will was published on 18 March; the funeral took place on 20 March; and Octavius did not arrive in Rome until May. In the play, the opening and the Lupercalia seem to precede by no more than a day Caesar's death, and thus occur on March 14; and the assassination, the funeral, the reading of the will and the arrival of Octavius – these all take place on March 15. (The compression results in "double time": at least one reference implies a longer time-scale than the obvious one: at 2.1.219, for instance, Brutus has had time to give Ligarius reasons for joining the conspiracy. In a traditional double-time scheme, as found in *Love's Labour's Lost*, *Othello* and *Measure for Measure*, the foreground action is rapid, but the background action is slower.) Historically, the Battle of Philippi had two phases separated by a 20-day interval; Shakespeare, however, lets both phases take place on the same day. Altogether, Shakespeare compresses three years into – apparently – a matter of days, perhaps a week or two. Shakespeare also reduces the number of locations, facilitating the stage-production: the triumvirs meet at Rome instead of near Bononia (later called Bologna).

Indeed, Shakespeare changed numerous parts of Plutarch's material in order to intensify the action, enrich characterisation, and heighten the ironies. Drama naturally tends to lend vivid immediacy to material which in such a source is merely a matter of report. Public rhetoric becomes more important in Shakespeare's version, being rendered in dramatic detail.

Colin Burrow says: "Above all Shakespeare took from the Greek Plutarch a sense of the *strangeness* of Rome". Shakespeare adopts, adapts and augments the supernatural events reported in the source-book, adding (for example) the lion that "glazed on" Caska at the Capitol. In Plutarch, a "horrible vision of a man" appears to Brutus ("I am thy ill angel, Brutus"); Shakespeare specifies that the ghost is that of Caesar, a crucial alteration which tightens the plot and retrospectively enhances Caesar's prestige. The apparition also retrospectively invests with irony Cassius's early remark, "'Brutus' will start a spirit as soon as 'Caesar'."

Shakespeare's additions to Plutarch include: the barrenness of Calphurnia, the character of Lucius, the detailed conduct of the common people, and the scene of the quarrel between Cassius and Brutus; and these additions obviously enrich the social, political and emotional aspects of the action.

Plutarch's Cassius, when explaining his Epicurean philosophy to Brutus, cites the belief that

we do not always feel or see that which we suppose we do both see and feel; ...our senses being credulous, and therefore easily abused...are induced to imagine they see and conjecture that which in truth they do not.

Robert S. Miola, again, comments:

This passage strikes the note of skepticism that resounds through the play, notably in Cicero's response to the portents: "But men may construe things after their fashion, / Clean from the purpose of the things themselves" (1.3.34-5). Throughout, the play demonstrates the delusory nature of the senses, the instability of judgement, the difficulty – nay, impossibility – of knowing rightly and judging truly.

The reader may reflect, "difficulty", yes; "impossibility", no, that's an exaggeration. After all, nobody could doubt that the mob which tore apart Cinna the poet was in the wrong. (We may feel that a better candidate for their wrath would have been the dire poetaster who intrudes on Brutus and Cassius in Act 4, scene 1.) Nevertheless, as Robert Miola says, interpretation and misinterpretation abound in the play: Caesar's character, the supernatural portents, Brutus's sleeplessness, Calphurnia's dream, the very assassination: all are subject to diverse scansion. Even Cassius's death is prompted by a misreading of the treatment of Titinius (who was being greeted, not captured).

Sometimes Shakespeare contradicted Plutarch. In Plutarch, Caesar distrusts the "pale visaged and carian [carrion] lean people", Cassius *and* Brutus, not Cassius alone. Plutarch's Cassius would "jest too broadly"; Shakespeare's Cassius, in marked contrast, is austere, hearing no plays and loving no music – always bad credentials in Shakespeare's world (they link him to Shylock and Malvolio; Brutus, in contrast, enjoys music). Shakespeare's crafty Cassius forges the citizens' letters to Brutus; in Plutarch, the letters are genuine. Plutarch's Brutus is worried by the

23

riskiness of the conspiracy, Shakespeare's by its morality. In Plutarch, Brutus and Cassius disagree about leading the right wing of the army: Shakespeare transfers this disagreement to Octavius and Antony (5.1.16-20), to portend their future strife, the lethal outcome depicted in *Antony and Cleopatra.*

Plutarch's Caesar tries repeatedly to read Artemidorus's warning, but cannot because of the crowds seeking to greet him; Shakespeare's Caesar, in contrast, nobly postpones consideration of it: "What touches ourself shall be last served." At the assassination, Plutarch's Casca calls for help in Greek – a language that Shakespeare's bluff, tough Caska cannot understand. The murder-location is dominated by the statue of Pompey; and Plutarch observes that here were "proofs that it was the ordinance of some god, that made this treason to be executed, specially in that very place": in other words, a god had ordained that Caesar, vanquisher of Pompey, should in turn be vanquished. Shakespeare's treatment is much more ambiguous.

Regarding the structure of the play, David Elloway, in his study of *Julius Caesar*, notes that Shakespeare has introduced a set of parallels between scenes.

The two night scenes, in Brutus's orchard and in his tent, are complementary...; the scene between Caesar and Calpurnia follows that between Brutus and Portia; the hot-blooded murder of Cinna is followed by the cold-blooded planning of murder by the Triumvirs, and the covert plotting of Antony against Lepidus by the open quarrel between Brutus and Cassius. Parallel scenes are sharply juxtaposed to provide and implicit comment on each other.

Robert Miola sums up:

Plutarch supplies the raw materials for this play, but Shakespeare assembles them into a distinctly modern vision of history – cynical and knowing, fully attuned to *Realpolitik* [political reality], devoid of illusion.

Repeatedly, Shakespeare in *Julius Caesar* seems to be saying: "Here's the public façade of politics; but don't be fooled: let's look *behind* the scenes, too, and see how people are deceived and manipulated. Furthermore, even the manipulators are subject to irony, the exposer of human limitations, as events tend to elude the endeavours of people to control them."

In this play, Shakespeare's view of politics is (predominantly though not entirely) sceptical and unillusioned: to that extent, *true*.

Contextualities: a medley of facts

1. According to Plutarch, Julius Caesar wrote *"Veni, vidi, vici"* ("I came, I saw, I conquered") after victory in his five-day war against Pharnaces II of Pontus. In *As You Like It*, Rosaline refers to Caesar's "thrasonical brag of 'I came, saw, and overcame'." (Thraso was a bragging character in Terence's play *Eunuchus*.) Between 1930 and 1960, a popular conga dance-tune had the title "I came, I saw, I conga'd".

2. Pliny the Elder estimated that Caesar had killed 1,192,000 enemies during his campaigns.

3. Two tribunes, Caius Epidius Marullus and Lucius Caesetius Flavus, ordered the removal of a royal diadem or headband from one of Caesar's statues in the Forum. Caesar condemned the men, but they were removed from office, not executed.

4. The name of the month of July honours Julius Caesar. In his lifetime, the Roman month of his birthday (previously called *"Quintilis"*, "month five") was renamed *"Julius"*.

3. The Latin adjective *brutus* means "stupid". The Brutus in *Julius Caesar* is a descendant of Lucius Junius Brutus (seen in *The Rape of Lucrece*), called "Brutus" because he feigned idiocy as a protective guise. (The name "Hamlet" derives from a word meaning "dimwit"; and Hamlet, too, for a while feigns idiocy.)

4. In Dante's *Inferno* (Canto XXXIV), Cassius is one of three men deemed so wicked that they are perpetually chewed in the three mouths of Satan: the other victims are Brutus and Judas Iscariot. Judas, betrayer of Jesus, is thus joined in ignominy by the betrayers of Julius Caesar. If St Matthew's gospel (27:5) is correct about Judas, all three committed suicide. Many Romans deemed suicide honourable; Roman Catholics deemed it a mortal sin.

5. Although modern editions of *Julius Caesar* usually give the name "Casca", the earliest source for Shakespeare's play, the First Folio (1623), spells it "Caska". The Latin alphabet has no letter "k". In the poem "To the Memory of my Beloved, the Author, Mr. William Shakespeare: and what he hath left us", Ben Jonson alleges "thou hadst small Latine, and lesse Greeke".

6. The Lupercalia, an annual fertility festival at Rome, has a name which derives from Lupercal and may derive ultimately from "lupus" – "wolf". Lupa was the name of the female wolf which suckled Romulus and Remus, legendary founders of Rome. Lupercal was a Roman god, the counterpart of the Greek Pan, a deity of fertility. During the Lupercalia, men wearing only hide loincloths would run through the city flicking people with goatskin whips: women struck by them were thought to become fertile. The historic Antony was once the leader of the runners.

7. Having ordained the reconstruction of Rome, Octavius later boasted that he found Rome brick and

left it marble: "*Urbem lateritiam invenit, marmoream reliquit.*"

8. St Luke's gospel (2:1) says that Octavius, as the emperor Caesar Augustus, issued the decree which obliged Joseph to take his pregnant wife Mary to Bethlehem to be recorded for taxation.

9. Michelangelo sculpted a bust of Brutus to commemorate the assassination of the tyrannical Alessandro de' Medici.

10. In Leonardo Vinci's baroque opera, *Catone in Utica* (1728), the role of Cesare (Julius Caesar) was originally sung by a castrato. In 2015, Franco Fagioli, the noted Argentinian counter-tenor, enjoyed great success as Cesare.

11. In Bertolt Brecht's play *Der aufhaltsame Aufstieg des Arturo Ui* (*The Resistible Rise of Arturo Ui*, 1941), the eponymous gangster-Führer takes elocution lessons from a veteran actor who, for the purpose, uses Antony's speech to the crowd in *Julius Caesar*.

12. In 2012, in London, an all-black production of *Julius Caesar*, directed by Gregory Doran, was staged by the Royal Shakespeare Company; and an all-female production, directed by Phyllida Lloyd, was staged at the Donmar Warehouse.

13. Prince Hamlet speculates that Julius Caesar may have become mere clay to fill a hole in a wall. In 2015, a parody of Mark Antony's speech beginning

"Friends, Romans, countrymen" was used in a televised advertisement for Jacob's Cracker Crisps.

Chapter 2: Genre and characterisation

Critics on *Julius Caesar*

> The many-headed multitude were drawne
> By *Brutus* speach, that *Caesar* was ambitious,
> When eloquent *Mark Antonie* had showne
> His vertues, who but *Brutus* then was vicious?
> (John Weever: *The Mirror of Martyrs*, 1601.)

[Shakespeare's] wit was in his owne power; would the rule of it had beene so too. Many times hee fell into those things, could not escape laughter: As when hee said in the person of *Caesar*, one speaking to him; *Caesar thou dost me wrong.* Hee replied: *Caesar did never wrong but with just cause:* and such like, which were ridiculous.
>   (Ben Jonson: *Discoveries*, 1641.)

> Our author by experience finds it true,
> 'Tis much more hard to please himself than you...
> But spite of all his pride, a secret shame
> Invades his breast at *Shakespear*'s sacred name:
> Aw'd when he hears his Godlike *Romans* rage,
> He, in a just despair, would quit the Stage;
> And to an Age less polish'd, more unskill'd,
> Does, with disdain, the foremost Honours yield.
> (John Dryden: "Prologue" to *Aureng-Zebe*, 1676.)

The whole design of the conspirators to liberate their country fails from the generous temper and over-weening confidence of Brutus in the goodness of their cause and the assistance of others. Thus it has always been. Those who mean well themselves think well of others, and fall a prey to their security. That humanity and honesty which dispose men to resist injustice and tyranny render them unfit to cope with the cunning and power of those who are opposed to them.

(William Hazlitt: *Characters of Shakespear's Plays*, 1817.)

[On Shakespeare's depiction of Caesar:] It is impossible for even the most judicially minded critic to look without a revulsion of indignant contempt at this travestying of a great man as a silly braggart, whilst the pitiful gang of mischief-makers who destroy him are lauded as statesmen and patriots... Regarded as a crafty stage job, the play is a triumph: rhetoric, claptrap, effective gushes of emotion, all the devices of the popular playwright, are employed with a profusion of power that almost breaks their backs.

(George Bernard Shaw: in a review of Beerbohm Tree's production of *Julius Caesar* in 1898. See *Shaw on Shakespeare*, 1962.)

[On the play as a whole:] Among its qualities...I shall single out only one – its moral and political realism....Whatever may be the ideological veneer, murder remains murder. There are greater and more complex things in Shakespeare, but there is nothing which better displays clarity and sanity of moral vision than Act III of *Julius Caesar*, with Brutus's

31

high-minded sacrificial attitude towards murder displayed without comment and condemning itself simply by expressing itself.

(J. C. Maxwell: "Shakespeare: The Middle Plays" in *The Age of Shakespeare*, ed. Boris Ford, 1955.)

[On *Julius Caesar* and *Coriolanus*:] They point to two related truths of the greatest importance. The first is that human actuality is more important than *any* political abstraction, though more difficult to bear. The second is that politics is vitiated and corrupted to the extent to which, as politicians, we lose our sense of the *person* on the other side of the dividing line of class or party or nation.

(L. C. Knights: "Shakespeare and Political Wisdom" in *Twentieth Century Interpretations of "Julius Caesar"*, ed. Leonard F. Dean, 1968.)

Soul...is absent from the Roman plays, naturally absent.

(John Bayley: *Shakespeare and Tragedy*, 1981.)

It is not necessary to be a Marxist or new historicist to appreciate that when first performed the impact of this play was potentially explosive. Here authority, and the contention for political power, are thoroughly interrogated...

(Vivian Thomas: *Julius Caesar*, 1992.)

In this play, on which Shakespeare had staked so much, either you fail to win your audience over and you die, or you stir them up and they tear a poet apart.

(Colin Burrow in *Around the Globe*, 2014.)

What is the genre of *Julius Caesar?*

As soon as you try to answer that question, you find that *Julius Caesar* can be located in a variety of genres; and, what's more, you then see that it becomes promptly responsive: it moves and changes, co-operatively re-arranging itself, in response to our choice of generic location. *The chosen generic context transforms the evident dramatic content.* Indeed, Vivien Thomas claims that "it is a play which challenges the very concept of genre". But, to perceive that challenge, we must first *utilise* the "very concept of genre".

Julius Caesar can be perceived as a *political history play*, and accordingly its relationship to Shakespeare's second tetralogy, *Richard II, Henry IV Parts 1 and 2*, and *Henry V*, becomes prominent. We then realise that the ethics of rebellion, a recurrent topic in all Shakespeare's English history plays hitherto, are being resumed with new sophistication and adroitness. The greatest political evil in a state, we are reminded, is civil war; and people whose acts instigate a civil war are usually punished. Furthermore, in that second tetralogy, Shakespeare had developed the technique of ambiguous characterisation which *Julius Caesar* presents with masterly skill.

Julius Caesar can also be seen as a *Roman play*, and in particular as part of the sequence of Shakespeare's plays in which Rome features as a setting. When we then link *Julius Caesar* to the previous *Titus Andronicus* and to the subsequent *Antony and Cleopatra* and *Coriolanus*, we see how some concepts which Shakespeare attributed to leading Romans are being explored and tested: notably, the concepts of patriotism, stoical heroism and noble self-awareness. Shakespeare's narrative poem *The Rape of Lucrece* augments the context, featuring the expulsion of Tarquin (and the ending of the monarchy) by Junius Brutus. *Julius Caesar* and *Antony and Cleopatra* can be seen as forming one great drama: the story of Antony and Octavius becomes "transtextual": we see how their story is concluded ironically (the defender of a Caesar being defeated by a Caesar), and how Roman virtues are contrasted with Egyptian pleasures: the ethical is challenged by the hedonistic and indeed by the ontological – by sheer fulness of being. (A "transtextual" narrative extends across two or more texts; if we know only one of its texts, we misjudge it. The story of Hal, later Henry V, extended over *four* texts.)

Another possible genre for *Julius Caesar* is obviously that of *tragedy*: after all, its original title – in the First Folio's Tragedy section – was *The Tragedie of Ivlivs Cæsar*; and then its location in Shakespeare's long sequence of tragedies comes to the fore. A theme of *Romeo and Juliet*, love destroyed by futile strife, recurs in *Julius Caesar*, partly in the killing of Caesar by Brutus, who loved him, and partly in the death of Portia, pining for Brutus. Arguably, Mercutio's cry, "A plague o' both your houses!" (said of the Mountagues and Capulets in *Romeo and Juliet*) could be applied to the successive combatants in *Julius Caesar*. We also see how *Julius Caesar* anticipates the next play in that sequence, *Hamlet*. Brutus's indecision anticipates in some ways

Hamlet's. *Hamlet*, in turn, will make numerous references to Julius Caesar (a role once played by Polonius, who will also be violently slain). The Prince, for example, sardonically recites to his friend Horatio:

Imperious Caesar, dead and turned to clay,
Might stop a hole to keep the wind away.
O, that that earth, which kept the world in awe,
Should patch a wall t'expel the winter's flaw!

[5.1]

In *Julius Caesar*, one could discern a tragedy with no fewer than three protagonists: the first being Caesar, the second and third being Brutus and Cassius. A "protagonist" is a main character; he or she may be opposed by an "antagonist"; but, as we see in the play, the antagonist may also become, in turn, another protagonist, encountering another antagonist. A classic tragic plot is crucially ironic: the protagonist embarks on a course which he believes will lead to success, but which, ironically, leads him to disaster. (Oedipus, for instance, seeks to save Thebes by identifying the killer of Laius; but he finds that the killer was himself.) Aristotle said that tragedy at best includes *peripeteia* and *anagnorisis*: the former being an ironic turn of events, so that the effect attained is the opposite to that intended; the latter being recognition of that irony by a protagonist. Caesar heads to the Senate House, expecting to be honoured with a crown; too late, he recognises that his progress has brought him to the lethal ambush. Brutus and Cassius, in turn, find that their plot has brought not success but their downfall, and they

35

acknowledge Caesar's hand in their malign destiny. Shakespeare thus achieves a triple co-ordination of *peripeteia* and *anagnorisis*, which in turn generates a large-scale pattern of ironies.

Kenneth Muir maintained that there is "no evidence that Shakespeare regarded the Roman plays as different *in kind* from the other tragedies". Vivien Thomas opposes this view, arguing that "tragedies leave us with a profound sense of finality, whereas the history plays [including the Roman plays] convey a sense of continuity". Her distinction, though useful, is too clear-cut. In Shakespeare's day, the term "tragedy" was used capaciously: *Richard II*, a history, was termed a tragedy; *Troilus and Cressida* was termed a tragedy *and* a history; and even *King Lear*, though designated a tragedy in the First Folio, was declared a history in the First Quarto. Within a work which evokes a sense of continuity, we can still select a tragic sequence: arguably this approach works for *Richard II* and *Julius Caesar*. David Elloway says of *Julius Caesar*:

As a whole the play reveals the moral complexity of political action, in which even the most well-meaning man is likely to go astray; indeed, that it is his very virtues that lead him astray: it is this that makes *Julius Caesar* a tragedy.

Another genre which solicits *Julius Caesar* is that of *revenge drama*. As in *The Spanish Tragedy* or *Titus Andronicus*, a victim is slain, and vengeance pursues the slayers. Here Antony and Octavius pursue and slay the killers of Caesar. A pattern of revenge can be seen; and Cassius clearly sees it: "Caesar, thou art revenged," he says, dying. But a big objection soon arises. The main objection to terming *Julius Caesar* a revenge drama is simply that the play is *too good*. The term "revenge drama" has, in course of time, usually become reserved for works which, though they may be vigorous and vivid, lack the depth or subtlety of works we call tragedies. If we are thinking *casually* about genres, bearing in mind the rough-and-ready categorisation of plays as tragedies, comedies or histories (as in the First Folio), then we may term *Titus Andronicus* a tragedy; but if we are giving *scrutiny* to terminology and refining the generic categories, then *Titus Andronicus* clearly belongs to the genre of revenge drama. In contrast: in its structure, *Hamlet* is a revenge drama, but it seems demeaning to call it such; "tragedy", being when scrutinised an honorific term (implying that such a work is powerful and profound), is more appropriate. So it is with *Julius Caesar*.

Here's yet another option. *Julius Caesar* could be placed in the genre of the "*problem play*". Ernest Schanzer wrote a critical volume entitled *The Problem Plays of Shakespeare: A Study of "Julius Caesar", "Measure for Measure", "Antony and Cleopatra"*. You might well say, "*What? Only three?*". (E. M. W. Tillyard, in *Shakespeare's Problem Plays*, had made a different selection: he put *Measure for Measure* alongside *Hamlet, Troilus and Cressida* and *All's Well That Ends Well*.) There are few plays of Shakespeare which cannot, by a moderately resourceful critic, be rendered problematic; and the absence of the notoriously problematic *Hamlet* from Schanzer's list seems perverse. But he was surely correct to include *Julius Caesar*.

37

He defines a problem play as one in which a central moral problem is presented in such a way that "we are unsure of our moral bearings, so that uncertain and divided responses to it in the minds of the audience are possible and even probable". In *Julius Caesar*, a central problem is the murder of Caesar: was it justified or not? (As David Daniell puts it: "Was it a necessary culling to save Rome? – King Henry V would have had no hesitation. Or was it, as Goethe called it, the most senseless deed that ever was done?") In a problem play, furthermore, claims Schanzer, the dramatist practises "dramatic coquetry", by which prominent characters variously engage and alienate our affections. Schanzer says that in *Julius Caesar* "our response to all four main characters, Caesar, Cassius, Antony, and even Brutus, is thus manipulated". He is surely correct, as a subsequent section of this chapter demonstrates. (Therefore Bertolt Brecht's famed *Verfremdungs-effekten* – alienation devices that make us react critically to what we see on stage – are at least as old as *Julius Caesar*.)

Thus, the answer to the question "Which genre for *Julius Caesar*?" gradually emerges. It is: "As many as prove fruitful". We might even invent a new genre for it: "*symphonic drama*", discussed in a later section. If we consider how the play may fit various genres, such consideration usefully reveals different facets of the work. It is not necessary to think that the play must have only one final generic location: *Julius Caesar* invites and encourages a variety of perspectives, and, in the theatre, it has naturally undergone diverse interpretations. Indeed, this drama is craftily designed to *solicit* such a diversity. Generically, the play is protean.

Who is the hero?

Much critical ink used to be expended on the question, "Who is the hero of *Julius Caesar*?". That the play is called *Julius Caesar* does not necessarily present the answer. Caesar is slain in Act 3, sc. 1, and he has far fewer lines than Brutus, Cassius or Antony. On the other hand, he "lives on" after his assassination: he appears as a ghost to Brutus, and both Brutus and Cassius acknowledge eventually that they have been defeated by the spirit of Caesar.

Brutus, however, is, according to his foe, Antony, "the noblest Roman of them all"; and some critics have argued that he is the true hero of the work. "Brutus is evidently the protagonist", asserted John Gielgud. Brutus has more lines than any other character. David Elloway claims: "He is the only character who suffers an internal conflict and into whose mind we are admitted so that we can share it." Elloway, however, adds: "In Shakespeare's greatest tragedies, by the end of the play the hero has learnt from his suffering. But Brutus has learnt nothing." Nevertheless, it is notable that numerous stage-productions (particularly in the USA, hospitable to apparent champions of liberty) have depicted Brutus as the hero.

In turn, Cassius is, according to David Daiches, "the co-hero of the play": he is the eloquent instigator of the plot, he reveals a poignant fallibility in his quarrel with Brutus, and his last act before dying is to liberate his slave, Pindarus. (Another irony: this champion of liberty has been a slave-owner.)

How about Antony? He emerges powerfully towards the end of the play, a master-orator and manipulator of people. In Daiches' view, Antony is "too good to be a tragic villain, too bad to be a tragic hero." But the actor-impresario Beerbohm Tree made Antony the most important character.

Caesar, Brutus, Cassius, Antony: in particular stage-productions, each of these has become the dominant character, the dominance often aided by cuts or even additions to the text. When Shakespeare wrote *Julius Caesar*, he, being a practical man of the theatre (actor, shareholder, playwright, and inevitably director, although the term "director" was not then used), knew that he was creating "the Julius Caesar material for the use of players": material to be cut, re-arranged and diversely interpreted as occasion demanded and the actors' abilities suggested. Generally, he seems to have relished such changeability. Hamlet is eager to add material to *The Mousetrap*, to make it trap Claudius more tightly; and, when Polonius complains that a speech is too long, Hamlet replies "It shall to the barber's, with your beard."

So, when we consider that body of textual material for *Julius Caesar*, a shrewder question than "Who is the hero?" would be: "Why do we feel puzzled when asked to nominate the hero of this play? "; or, "Why does it seem to falsify the nature of the play if we seek just *one* protagonist?". The answer is obvious: in *Julius Caesar*, as represented in the Folio text, the interest lies in a sequence of events to which several important characters make essential contributions; but the significance lies in the enacted sequence, not centrally in any one figure at all. Julius Caesar may well be the most important of those characters, but to designate him "the hero" or "the protagonist" may well distort the nature of this play, which deals with a richly political and moral sequence of events. In Bertolt Brecht's *Leben des Galilei* (*The Life of Galileo*, 1955), Galileo says: "Unhappy the land that is in need of heroes." In *Julius Caesar*, for all the tributes offered to Caesar, Cassius and Brutus, Shakespeare anticipates Galileo's assertion by several centuries.

"The play is not about Caesar or Cassius or Brutus; it is about the high and palmy state of Rome", asserts Muriel Bradbrook. "The main character is the audience", suggests actor Luke Thompson. To Bradbrook, we may respond: "But the state of Rome, as shown, is not always high (as Cinna the poet might attest) and certainly not 'palmy' (i.e. flourishing). for it is riven and civil war impends; and it is defined by reference to the fates of the particular characters." To Thompson, we may respond: "The play certainly involves the audience to a greater extent than is customary in Shakespearian drama; and the audience is made unusually conscious of its judicial function. Of course, the audience is co-ordinator of the action; but that, though true, is trivial, since the audience, if responsive, acts as co-ordinator of *any* stage production, endeavouring to make coherent sense of what is perceived; and the audience of *Julius Caesar* is likely, in any case, to be markedly divided in evaluation of the events depicted."

Although particular productions for stage or screen may make one character dominate (and often they do), the original Folio text of *Julius Caesar* is that of an ensemble-drama, perhaps even a symphonic drama. Later, in *Troilus and Cressida*, Shakespeare will extend yet further the concept of a play dominated by its process, co-ordinated by its thematic clusters and its unfolding ironic pattern: the characters are essential to the exposition but, while expressing its themes, are subordinate to the design: fully symphonic drama, rich in deliberate discords. "And hark, what discord follows", says Ulysses, predicting a breakdown of order; and that breakdown is expressed in the very structure of *Troilus and Cressida* itself, with its ostentatiously disorderly conclusion. There we encounter symbolic malformation: ordered disorder.

In *Julius Caesar* we see an undulant pattern of recurrent rise and fall: ostensibly great men are repeatedly superseded: after Pompey, Caesar; after Caesar, Brutus and Cassius; after them, Antony and Octavius; and, in *Antony and Cleopatra*, the pattern will continue and be completed with the fall of Antony.

If we look again at Schanzer's concept of "dramatic coquetry", we soon realise that it did not suddenly emerge with *Julius Caesar*. In *Richard II*, Shakespeare had used such coquetry in the depiction of Richard himself, who was variously majestic, imperious, callous, cynical, self-pitying, self-dramatising, pathetic, defiant and courageous. (Shakespeare had studied and partly copied Christopher Marlowe's brilliant portrayal of the rapidly-changeable Edward II.) To a lesser extent, Bolingbroke in that play was ambiguous, being astute, defiant, brave, crafty, hypocritical, worried and burdened. And the action of *Richard II*, we then see, strongly portended *Julius Caesar*; for *Richard II*

43

dealt with a conspiracy against a ruler, a conspiracy culminating in assassination and a political takeover; and that in turn resulted in bloody and protracted civil war.

It's a similar pattern in *Julius Caesar*: Shakespeare is fascinated by the way in which the death of an individual can lead to a national disaster: an action of apparently limited scope having consequences vaster – and worse – than the initiators of the action can have imagined. Here are lessons (too often ignored) for politicians. For instance, in recent times, the west's military actions against Saddam Hussein in Iraq and against Muammar Gaddafi in Libya led not to emergent democracy but to protracted and chaotic sectarian violence in those regions.

Symphonic drama, inaugurated by Aeschylus

Aeschylus showed the way, when composing *The Oresteia* (458 B.C.). In that trilogy, at first the centre of interest is Agamemnon, who is slain; then the central position is held by Clytemnestra, his slayer; next, it's Orestes, slayer of Clytemnestra; next, the court of the Areopagus; and, eventually, Athens itself. The individuals, subordinated to the whole, like soloists voicing the themes within a symphony, have contributed to a drama about the evolution of justice, and, indeed, of civilisation. Justice based on the law of talion ("an eye for an eye, and a tooth for a tooth"), which threatens to become an endless pattern of vengeance and counter-vengeance, is superseded by justice dispensed by a court of law, which can take account of individual circumstances, mitigating factors, and the good of society at large. From vindictive barbarism emerge law and order and civilised democracy.

In *Julius Caesar*, the individuals form part of a drama about the morality of rebellion and political "direct action", and about the tensions between the public and the private, and between ideology and individuality. To ask "Who is the hero of *Julius Caesar?*" is a necessary question, precisely because it leads us to perceive the elusiveness of a simple answer. As we then recognise the ambivalence of the characterisations, and the fallibilities of all the leading figures, we see that what matters predominantly is the discussion to which they contribute: the greater whole of which they form contributory parts; a whole which is informed by morally-directed ironies. And such coordinated complexity invites the analogy with a symphony.

Whereas *The Oresteia* has a strongly positive, even festive, conclusion, the ending of *Julius Caesar* is relatively muted. The assassins have met harsh justice, and their avenging foes have prevailed; but, though Octavius speaks of "the glories of this happy day", there remains a sense of waste, and there is no assurance that the rule of Antony and Octavius will be harmonious.

The Aeschylean trilogy was completed by a fourth play, *Proteus*, which, though lost, would have been a short farcical play offering comic relief after the previous tragic events. The dance concluding *Julius Caesar* (in the 1599 version seen by Thomas Platter, described later, and in, for example, the 2014 production at Shakespeare's Globe Theatre) is a counterpart to the ancient convention of the satyr play which follows a tragic sequence.

How does Shakespeare manipulate our responses to the main characters?

1. Julius Caesar

If we ask, "Was the assassination of Caesar justified?", we are led to search Caesar's character; and Shakespeare has made it complex and subtle.

From ancient times to Shakespeare's, Julius Caesar had been a controversial figure, dividing the commentators. He could be seen as great leader *and* ambitious egoist, while Brutus could be seen as virtuous republican *and* deluded murderer. Cicero and others admired Caesar's abilities but criticised his ambitions. Dio Cassius's *Roman History* condemned his killers as frenzied envious men. Gaius Velleius Paterculus praised Caesar as a transcendent genius of divine descent. Lucan's *Pharsalia* depicted him as a force of destruction. Chaucer in *The Monk's Tale* deplored his murder by "This false Brutus and his othere foon [foes]". John Stow's *Chronicle* (1580) declared Caesar "the most ambitious and greatest traitor that ever was to the Roman state". Montaigne praised Caesar's talents but deemed his "pestilential" ambition disastrous.

In the play, the conspirators' main allegation against Caesar is that he is gaining autocratic power and seeks to be king. This would mean the end of republican Rome and a return to the days when a royal dynasty ruled – an era that Brutus's ancestor, Lucius Junius Brutus, had helped to end. (Plutarch had spoken of Caesar's "covetous desire...to be called king".) Caska reports that at the Lupercalian ceremonies, Antony offered Caesar a crown, and Caesar (to the crowd's acclaim) declined it – but reluctantly, according to Caska. Evidently Caesar knows how to manipulate the emotions of the masses: in a bold histrionic gesture, he opens his doublet and "offer[s] them his throat to cut" – presumably as if to say, "I am your servant; kill me if I displease you". (Later, Antony will offer himself to the blades of the conspirators, and, ironically, Cassius will, in a similar gesture, offer himself to be killed by Brutus. "Death before dishonour" is a famous Roman trope.) It is notable that some of the most impressive tributes to Caesar come from his killers: to Brutus he is "the foremost man of all this world"; and Cassius declares: "Why, man, he doth bestride the narrow world / Like a Colossus" – a criticism which yet conveys his grandeur.

Certainly, the Caesar that we see is proudly egoistic, speaking of himself in the third person as though he were already a famous historical leader; even, at least half-deified. His fluency in self-aggrandizing magniloquence reaches its extreme when he says (defying the augurers who tell him not to venture forth):

> Danger knows full well
> That Caesar is more dangerous than he.
> We are two lions littered in one day,
> And I the elder and more terrible. [2.2]

Calphurnia tactfully responds:

> Alas, my lord,
> Your wisdom is consumed in confidence

– in other words, "Your confidence has overcome your wisdom", a polite way of indicating that his self-dramatisation now verges on lunacy: at the least, it displays the hubris (pride) that invites nemesis (retribution). He is certainly capable of fatal error, as when he dismisses the soothsayer's warning of the Ides of March, saying "He is a dreamer".

As we have noted, when Caesar is offered a petition which would have warned him of the conspiracy, his modesty ironically leads him to put it aside: "What touches ourself shall be last served." The concern of Artemidorus and the soothsayer, coupled with the demonstration by the commoners in scene 1, confirms that Cesar enjoys widespread popularity. (As A. D. Nuttall points out, citing the rise of Hitler, the play thus raises a problem for democrats: how to respond if the people choose autocracy.) Caesar can also be warmly and knowledgeably hospitable. When Publius and the conspirators call on him, he greets them individually, reproaches himself for keeping them waiting, and invites them in to take wine with him. He can also be sharply observant, even incisive, as when describing to Mark Antony the character of Cassius, with his "lean and hungry look".

Though imperious in manner, Caesar has physical frailties, being deaf in one ear: a symbolic ailment invented for him by Shakespeare. It is symbolic in implying that he is deaf to good advice. Caesar is also subject to the "falling sickness", evidently some form of epilepsy. Cassius says that though Caesar now seems to "bestride the narrow world / Like a Colossus", he, in the past, nearly drowned and was shaken by a bout of fever. If Cassius is truthful here, which may not be the case, the effect of his reports may actually be to make us the more impressed by Caesar's achievements notwithstanding such human frailties. Plutarch had said that during his successful martial campaigns, Caesar repeatedly endured hardship and triumphed over adversities. (By his victories, the real Caesar, who was brave and hardy, enriched Rome and himself by gaining loot, supplies, and slaves for sale.)

Caesar can be irresolute and vain: Calphurnia and the Soothsayer persuade him to stay at home instead of venturing forth into danger's way; but when a conspirator, Decius, reinterprets Calphurnia's ominous dream, says that the senators will offer him a crown, and adds that they will whisper "Caesar is afraid" if Caesar will not come, Caesar resolves to set out after all. Fatally, he gives public life priority over private loyalty: if love for Calphurnia had prevailed, he would have lived. It is one of the themes of the play: repeatedly political action subverts the claims of love, kinship and familial loyalty.

Caesar never sounds more impressive than in his final minutes (in Act 3, sc. 1), when the assassins surround him, ostensibly seeking a pardon for Metellus Cimber's banished brother. To their cynical bowing and flattery, Caesar responds:

> Be not fond
> To think that Caesar bears such rebel blood
> That will be thawed from the true quality
> With that which melteth fools: I mean, sweet
>   words,
> Low-crookèd curtsies and base spaniel fawning.

Here we see a famous Shakespearian associative cluster: sweets, melting, spaniels, fawning. In *Antony and Cleopatra* (Act 4, scene 12), Antony, feeling betrayed, will say:

>   The hearts
> That spanieled me at heels...
>   ...do discandy, melt their sweets
> On blossoming Caesar...

This image-cluster, first studied by Walter Whiter in 1794, is a unique thumb-print of Shakespeare's imagination (as Caroline Spurgeon explained in her book, *Shakespeare's Imagery*, 1935): it expresses deeply-felt disgust; and here it intensifies Caesar's scorn.

When Brutus and Cassius continue the plea, Caesar rises to a height of eloquence:

> I could be well moved, if I were as you;
> If I could pray to move, prayers would move me.
> But I am constant as the Northern Star,
> Of whose true fixed and resting quality
> There is no fellow in the firmament.
> The skies are painted with unnumbered sparks;
> They are all fire, and every one doth shine;
> But there's but one in all doth hold his place.
> So in the world: 'tis furnished well with men,
> And men are flesh and blood, and apprehensive;
> Yet, in the number, I do know but one
> That unassailable holds on his rank,
> Unshaked of motion; and, that I am he... [3.1]

Of course, he is here displaying proud egotism; but the majesty of utterance serves to validate his pride: who else but Caesar could talk like this? His rhetoric, in contrast to the pleading of the conspirators, helps to validate the sense that Caesar is indeed like the Northern Star, the Pole Star, not only in constancy but in ascendancy – above the average of men of "flesh and blood". Certainly he sounds autocratic; but impressively so; and he is displaying courage here, too, in his defiance of the numerous pressing suitors. So persuasively confident is the rhetoric that we may forget that, a few minutes ago, far from being "constant as the Northern Star", he had dithered about whether to set out for the Senate or not. He claims to be "unshaked", this man who is subject to the "falling sickness". And this "unassailable" figure is about to be assailed.

The assassins now strike him down; and his last words are words of reproach and resignation: "*Et tu, Brute*? – Then fall, Caesar!*". One man, unarmed and no longer young (the historic Caesar being about 56 when slain), is slaughtered by numerous armed men. It would be a very unusual production in which our sense of "fair play" and elementary morality were not evoked against the assassins and in favour of their victim.

This victim, however, can strike back posthumously: he reappears as vengeful ghost, and Brutus and Cassius endorse his posthumous power. Cassius's last words are: "Caesar, thou art revenged, / Even with the sword that killed thee" – the sword that "ran through Caesar's bowels". Brutus, on finding Cassius's body, declares: "O Julius Caesar, thou art mighty yet"; and, when dying, Brutus says, "Caesar, now be still; I killed not thee with half so good a will." When seeking to turn Brutus against Caesar, Cassius had claimed that "'Brutus' will start a spirit as soon as 'Caesar'." The American critic Harold Bloom rightly remarks that this line is highly ironic, "since the Ghost of Caesar will identify himself as 'Thy evil spirit, Brutus'."

Indeed, it is Caesar's posthumous presence, and the scale of the strife consequent on his assassination, which endorses the merit of the Caesar who once lived. The play may thus seem "the tragedy of a great leader martyred". Caesar's stature has repeatedly been exalted by the numerous supernatural portents: there wouldn't be all these weird and amazing events (lion in the Capitol, man with hand on fire, "exhalations" – comets – lighting the skies, etc.) for the impending death of a mere commoner. As Calphurnia rightly observes: "When beggars die, there are no comets seen". *Metaphysical mayhem magnifies the leader, and his appearance as ghost verifies his immortality.* Shakespeare provides crucial "mystification" of a magnate. (We may recall that Shakespeare's Richard II, though a flawed ruler, truly predicted the wars that ensued after his downfall; and the very fact that he predicted truly added retrospectively to his stature: posthumously, he gained the aura of a prophet.) When directed by John Schlesinger at the National Theatre in London in 1977, John Gielgud's Caesar "had such great natural authority that his spirit was obviously unconquerable from the start", reports David Daniell.

A common but lazy assumption of commentators is that by the time of a character's death, we have accumulated all the information we need to assess that character. That assumption is clearly, in the case of Caesar, erroneous. By his posthumous presence, Caesar is exalted. He is given power to visit, haunt and ultimately destroy (or aid the destruction of) his enemies. He thereby gains powerful moral vindication. Being an agent in a moral victory over his assassins, he thereby casts a retrospectively exalting light upon his character as it appeared before his assassination. The ghost projects charisma back in time to irradiate his flesh-and-blood progenitor: we witness an enhancive symbiosis of wraith and man.

It also affects our judgement of Caesar that the leader of the conspiracy against him has some Machiavellian characteristics: Cassius, remember, forges letters to give Brutus the false impression that the hostility to Caesar is more widespread than is the case; and, later, in the famous quarrel scene (4.2), we learn that Cassius is open to charges of corruption – charges which Cassius does not refute.

On the other hand, even the depiction of Caesar as avenging ghost does not curtail the ambivalence of the characterisation. For example: modern stage productions have often associated Caesar with such dictators as Hitler and Mussolini. When Caesar first enters the play, autocratic features are evident. Immediately after he calls "Calphurnia", Caska shouts, "Peace, ho! Caesar speaks." When Antony is given instructions by Caesar, Antony's sycophantic response is "When Caesar says 'Do this', it is performed." And when the soothsayer calls to him, Caesar does not say, "Speak: I am listening"; he says "Speak, Caesar is turned to hear" – referring to himself in the third person, thereby invoking himself as a historic personage. When Caska reports the theatrical performance of Caesar before the applauding masses, we may distantly be reminded of Hitler's Nuremberg rallies. The information that Caesar's critics, Flavius and Murellus, have been "put to silence" suggests that Caesar's rule is supported by ruthlessly efficient agents. (In some productions, Flavius and Murellus are seized and hauled away from the procession opening Act 1, sc. 2.)

Famously, Orson Welles's 1937 production in New York of *Julius Caesar*, sub-titled *Death of a Dictator*, gave the play obvious topicality. In this free adaptation, the drama concerned "the catastrophic failure of the liberal, faced with the ruthless force of Fascism. Caesar was Mussolini and some settings were Nazi rallies" (notes Daniell). Costumes included street clothes and fascist uniforms. Caesar wore a cross-belted military tunic and riding-breeches; Antony's eulogy of Caesar was offset by vertical searchlights, evoking a Nazi Nuremberg rally. The uniformed Caesar was greeted by Fascist salutes from his supporters. This version of the play was acclaimed and had a long run of 157 performances. (It prompted the 2009 film, *Me and Orson Welles*.)

Subsequent stage productions have sometimes treated Caesar as a Latin American dictator; and in 1986, in a production at Miami (home to numerous Cuban exiles), he resembled Fidel Castro. On Terry Hands' 1987 production at the Royal Shakespeare Company, the critic Michael Billington astutely commented: "If Caesar is so nakedly Fascist, does it not detract from Brutus' moral qualms about his murder?". At the Barons' Court Theatre in London in 1993, Caesar was played by a woman, to associate the leader with Margaret Thatcher. Arthur Humphreys offers a warning: "The more relevance, the less resonance... Shakespeare himself takes no sides, or all sides."

Richard II appears in some ways conservative (the killing of the monarch is a shocking event); yet the Earl of Essex's supporters thought that it helped their rebellious cause, and arranged a special performance of it before their revolt against Queen Elizabeth in 1601. Shakespeare knew well, by the time he wrote *Julius Caesar*, that a good text could be protean in relevance. The marked differences between the early texts of *Hamlet* (the first quarto offering a much shorter version than the second, and the second differing significantly from what is found in the First Folio) show that plays could take on markedly different forms at different locations. Shakespeare was indeed creating "the Julius Caesar material for the use of players", and over the centuries it has repeatedly reflected (or has been inflected to reflect) the political concerns of the times.

2. Brutus

In Ben Jonson's *Sejanus* (1603), Brutus and Cassius are hailed as noble Romans who opposed "evil" Caesar. From the 17th century onwards, a strong tradition in the theatre has depicted Brutus as a noble republican fighting a despotic tyrant. Thomas Betterton, the greatest actor of the late 17th century, played Brutus as a "majestic philosophical stoic": Arthur Humphreys says:

Betterton made the play predominantly Brutus', and its tenor that of protecting republican liberty against despotic encroachment. This remained its message through the first half of the eighteenth century, when it was very popular.

That was the period of the English "Augustan Age", when writers felt that the era resembled that of Augustus: after a costly civil war, there emerged a stable era in which the arts could flourish.

This tradition, Brutus as hero, then became very powerful in the United States. The text was customarily trimmed to fit notions of Roman dignity: the lines about the conspirators staining their hands with Caesar's blood were often cut; Brutus's failings were reduced; Caesar became the dangerous autocrat; and Antony lost some unscrupulousness, as the proscription scene (4.1) was usually deleted.

David Daniell claims:

Young America of the Revolution took the libertarian passions of *Julius Caesar* to its soul (and commonplace books). The play was from the beginning of the United States a serious part of North American life for students, politicians, orators and all theatre people: it has been so ever since.

The first American production was on 1 June 1770 in Philadelphia, where the advertisement proclaimed "The noble struggles for Liberty by that renowned patriot Marcus Brutus". A drama critic of the day praised *Julius Ceasar* "for the growing spirit of liberty it breathes [and its] elegant and sublime language". In the 18th and 19th centuries, numerous eminent American actors took the role: among them, Lewis Hallam, John Hodgkinson, Thomas Hamblin, Edward Davenport, Thomas Cooper, the Booths, William Augustus Conway and Edwin Forrest.

57

Daniell comments: "The republican ideal was high – indeed, the success of the new nation depended on it."

Since the U.S.A. was born in a rebellion against a monarchy, you can at once see why Brutus was so appealing to Americans. But in England, too, Brutus was the dominant character in stage productions for at least two centuries. (At the "Glorious Revolution" of 1688, the autocratic King James II had been expelled; nobody sought a return to autocratic rule.) The actor-manager John Kemble altered the text so that the play became the tragedy of Brutus, the great patriot, whose last speech now included the added words "Thus Brutus strikes his last – for liberty!". In the late 19th century, however, there came increasing respect for the ambivalences in Shakespeare's characterisations. In the 20th century, as we have seen, there was a tendency for Caesar to be depicted as a totalitarian dictator and Brutus as the liberal opposing him. In that Orson Welles production, Brutus's plight was "truly tragic,...the destruction of virtuousness by the logic of its own virtue" , said Archibald MacLeish, reviewing it in *The Nation*, 4 December 1938.

In Shakespeare's characterisation of Brutus, the salient features are his reputation for uprightness of character, his nobility and integrity, but also his flawed judgment. Antony terms him "noble, wise, valiant and honest"; but "wise" is obviously questionable; some of us may think the adjective quite inappropriate. Brutus misjudges Caska and Antony. Crucially, in a revealing soliloquy, Brutus deems Caesar worthy of assassination not for what he *is* (as "the quarrel / Will bear no colour for the thing he is") but for what he *may become*:

Fashion it thus: that what he is, augmented,
Would run to these and these extremities;
And therefore think him as a serpent's egg
(Which, hatched, would as his kind grow
                                    mischievous),
And kill him in the shell. [2.1]

Brutus is talking himself into defending the indefensible: he is indeed "fashioning" the motive, contriving, shaping, and even – for this meaning is within the term's range – faking it. (His "serpent's egg" logic had a notorious subsequent illustration. In 2003, western politicians said that Saddam Hussein might use weapons of mass destruction in the future; therefore his country, Iraq, should be invaded in the present. The invasion took place; no such weapons were found; Hussein was eventually hanged; and the region became turbulent.) The critic Simon Palfrey observes of Brutus's reflections:

The soliloquy shows very explicitly the sort of wilfully jaundiced and manipulative rhetoric that will now run the civil wars.

Later, Brutus's endeavour to make the assassination dignified is mocked by the gory outcome. Every time Brutus successfully defies Cassius (notably in insisting that Antony be not slain and that he be allowed to make the funeral address), he helps to bring about disaster for the conspirators. Tactically, Cassius usually has the wisdom that Brutus lacks. When the civil war is being waged, it is Brutus who insists that the rebels proceed at once to battle at Philippi, whereas the shrewder Cassius argues that

> 'Tis better that the enemy seek us:
> So shall he waste his means, weary his soldiers,
> Doing himself offence; whilst we, lying still,
> Are full of rest, defence and nimbleness. [4.2]

But Brutus prevails, and disaster at Philippi follows. On the battlefield, by giving prematurely the word of victory, he sets his soldiers pillaging instead of aiding Cassius's failing army. A tragic pattern unfolds. The critic David Daiches remarks: "If Brutus had been a less simply virtuous man, he would not have helped to kill one of his best friends and brought tyranny to Rome (the opposite of what he intended)." Brutus has the Stoic's virtues and faults: the virtues including a noble sense of dignity and duty, the faults being an element of arrogance and of austerity inclining to coldness. Like Caesar, he sometimes uses third-person address for himself.

As a characterisation, Brutus is finely detailed: noble yet fallible; proud of his integrity yet weak in logic; seemingly independent yet hoodwinked by Cassius into joining the conspiracy. As in *Macbeth*, a protagonist commits a murder, only to find that the imagined benefits are denied him, so that disillusionment results. For an accomplished actor, the role of Brutus may well seem the most interesting and therefore attractive in the play; and indeed then the play may appear to be "the tragedy of a noble Roman misled".

The private self of Brutus is subtly and strongly rendered. After Cassius has told him of the conspiracy, Brutus is sleepless, reflecting:

Between the acting of a dreadful thing
And the first motion, all the interim is
Like a phantasma or a hideous dream...[2.1]

For a while, there, he sounds like Macbeth. Again, a revealing sequence appears when his wife, Portia, reproaches him for not letting her share his evident worries.

Dwell I but in the suburbs
Of your good pleasure? If it be no more,
Portia is Brutus' harlot, not his wife. [2.1]

Her protestation of loyalty to him is strongly "Romanised": she is proud of her marriage and of her lineage, being the daughter of Marcus Porcius Cato, a Roman statesman noted for integrity. He had fought for Pompey against Caesar, and had killed himself when Pompey was defeated. Furthermore, Portia has wounded herself in the thigh in order to prove to Brutus that she could bear and share pain: another stoically Roman gesture. "O ye gods!", Brutus exclaims, "Render me worthy of this noble wife!". He agrees to tell her his secrets. Later, however, Portia will commit suicide, partly because she deplores his absence as the civil war develops. (She "swallowed fire", putting burning coals in her mouth and choking. Plutarch explains that she preferred such a death to a painful illness: by eliding this explanation, Shakespeare accentuates her devotion to Brutus.) We are also shown Brutus's tender concern for his servant, the boy Lucius: affectionately considerate, he even, as the lad dozes, takes away his musical instrument, lest it fall and break: a telling detail, revealing Brutus at his kindly best and Shakespeare at his descriptive best – providing an unexpected and touching insight.

Brutus is loved by Caesar, Portia, Cassius, and perhaps by Lucius and fellow patricians. The scene of the quarrel between Brutus and Cassius (4.2) has long been regarded as one of the finest and most memorable scenes in the play; it ends in a moving reconciliation. Eventually, after a tellingly illogical passage of dialogue, Brutus kills himself with the aid of Strato. Before that, Brutus had told Cassius that he disapproved of Cato's suicide, regarding it as "cowardly and vile"; but when Cassius then enquired whether he was willing to be led as a captive back to Rome, Brutus (with remarkable inconsistency) said:

Think not, thou noble Roman,
That ever Brutus will go bound to Rome:
He bears too great a mind. [5.1]

Illogicality capped with self-praise. Consider: if he'd said, "*I* bear too great a mind", that would have been simple vanity; whereas, by speaking as though he is describing a different figure, Brutus as historical entity, he purports to be stating a fact – but a fact about a hubristic self-image. In his suicide, Brutus is granted the theatrical "accolade of the final death", the most prestigious character in a drama usually being the last to die. He then gains that remarkably generous posthumous tribute from Antony. Alone among the conspirators, says Antony, Brutus intended "common good to all":

> His life was gentle, and the elements
> So mixed in him that Nature might stand up
> And say to all the world, "This was a man!" [5.5]

"Gentle"? We remember his knife stabbing Caesar. And Brutus's mixture of elements certainly included a blinkered pride and permitted faulty judgements.

Daniell says of Brutus: "He is far more than just a flawed hero for later republicans. He is the first tragic hero with any significant interior life to appear in English drama." Harold Bloom declares: "Brutus is Shakespeare's first intellectual." Edward Dowden in 1872 said that Brutus "with each new error advances a fresh claim upon our admiration and our love". John Dover Wilson claimed in 1948 that the play amply confirms Brutus's reading of Caesar's character (in 2.1.10-34) as dangerously ambitious. But (as a reminder of the ambivalence of the Brutus's characterisation) Mark Van Doren has described Brutus as a character who has no flaws "except the dramatic one of an impenetrable and inexpressible nobility"; "the fine man is a coarse thinker, the saint of self-denial has little self to deny"; indeed,

Shakespeare has done all that could be done with such a man, but what could be done was limited. The hero is heavy in the poet's hands; his reticence prevents intimacy...

John Gielgud (who performed the part often enough) adds bluntly that Brutus "is entirely without humour and may easily seem dull and priggish".

Mark Antony declares Brutus "the noblest Roman of them all" because he slew Caesar "in a general honest thought", seeking "common good to all". A. D. Nuttall claims that there is "no irony" in this declaration, for Brutus always "tried to be good". As Coppélia Kahn observes, however, Mark Antony's words have an ironic context. Antony himself is motivated not by the general good but by vengefulness and ambition. His triumvirate rules "by fiat and terror". And

he envisions one man only in that republic who triumphs – in virtue – over all the over all the rest.

Arguably, however, that republic was already defunct: rendered defunct by the spirit of emulation and by the contempt displayed by the aristocrats towards the plebeians. As Wayne Rebhorn, a "New Historicist", has remarked, although Brutus regarded the assassination as a rejection of tyranny, "he, like Cassius, clearly feels a sense of having been degraded by Julius Caesar's rise". Indeed, Rebhorn continues,

The senators, in killing Caesar because of his emulous ambition, were really striking at the defining principle of their class. To put it most directly: Brutus, Cassius and the other conspirators *are* Caesar; in assassinating him, they are consequently plunging their swords symbolically into their own vitals even before they would literally do so at Philippi.

Within the supposedly noble character of Brutus, Nuttall notes signs of "a dark impulse to cruelty". For instance, Brutus says:

Let's be sacrificers, but not butchers, Caius...
Let's kill him boldly but not wrathfully;
Let's carve him as a dish fit for the gods... [2.1]

Brutus is commending moderation; but after the "manly simplicity" of "Let's kill him boldly", "Let's carve him as a dish" is "mildly troubling, slightly weird": it hints at that dark impulse to cruelty. Later, Brutus says:

> Stoop, Romans, stoop,
> And let us bathe our hands in Caesar's blood
> Up to the elbows, and besmear our swords;
> Then...
> Let's all cry "Peace, freedom and liberty!" [3.1]

Instead of cleansing away the pollution, washing with water, Brutus wants the conspirators to magnify the pollution. Nuttall concludes:

The ordinary horror of the blood makes Brutus sound almost schizophrenic: logical, imaginative, yet unaware of reality and driven by it in ways he does not comprehend.

(These comments bring to mind Harold Bloom's speculation that Brutus harbours Oedipal hostility to his fatherly ruler.)

The wounded Caesar's famous question, "*Et tu, Brute?*", bears detailed scrutiny. Those words mean, literally, "And thou, O Brutus?", or, more colloquially, "Even *you*, Brutus?". Caesar is registering the fact that the conspirators include a person whom Caesar would never have expected to raise a knife against him. On realising that Brutus, of

65

all people, is one of the assassins, Caesar accordingly resigns himself to death: "Then fall, Caesar!"

One reason for Caesar's surprise at encountering Brutus among his slayers is that Brutus is a dear friend as well as a noted man of honour. We know that the assassins thought it important to win Brutus to their cause, to ennoble it, and we know that it was only after an inner struggle that Brutus submitted to the conspirators' arguments.

Another, more personal and emotional reason for Caesar's surprise may be that Brutus is *his son*. Historians speculated that Brutus, whose mother, Servilia Caepionis, was Julius Caesar's favourite mistress, was Caesar's son. (If that were the case, Caesar would have been only 15 years old when Brutus was born; but that does not rule out paternity.) Shakespeare knew of this speculation: *Henry VI, Part 2,* says that Caesar was slain by "Brutus's bastard hand"; and, In *Julius Caesar*, Act 3, scene 2, Mark Antony's great oration to the Romans offers corroboration. Holding Caesar's mantle, Antony says:

> Through this the well-belovèd Brutus stabbed,
> And as he plucked his cursèd steel away,
> Mark how the blood of Caesar followed it,
> As rushing out of doors, to be resolved
> If Brutus so unkindly knocked, or no:
> For Brutus, as you know, was Caesar's angel.
> Judge, O you gods, how dearly Caesar loved him!
> This was the most unkindest cut of all...

Key-words here include "unkindly" and (in a notorious double superlative) "unkindest", as, for Shakespeare, these connote "unnaturally" and "most unnatural" – appropriate terms if Brutus was Caesar's son, of Caesar's blood; which, in turn, would explain why Brutus was "Caesar's angel", so dearly loved.

But why were the words "*Et tu, Brute?*" uttered in Latin? The original Romans would, of course, have conversed in Latin, sometimes in Greek. In the play, from the outset, we have accepted the standard convention that the Roman characters speak English. Probably Caesar breaks into Latin at this point because the Latin phrase was already well known to English readers. The phrase is quoted in *The True Tragedie of Richard, Duke of York*, 1595, the earliest printed version of Shakespeare's *Henry VI, Part 3*. Thinking that Clarence has betrayed him, King Edward says: "*Et tu, Brute? Wilt thou stab Caesar too?*". The readiness with which he applies the Latin to the situation suggests that the phrase was already familiar. It may have been first used in *Caesar Interfectus* [*Caesar Slain*], a tragedy in Latin performed in 1582. (That play, now lost, has been attributed to Richard Edes or Eedes.)

In his *De Vita Caesarum*, section 82, the famous Roman historian Suetonius says that others have claimed that Caesar's last words were a Greek phrase (which can be transliterated as "Kai su, teknon?") meaning "You too, youngster?" but interpretable, tellingly, as "You too, my child?". As we reflect on the implications of "my child", the assassination becomes more treacherous and becomes the most salient illustration of the ways in which the political opposes and even violates the personal. Often in this play, private harmony is disrupted by public commitment. Repeatedly, political ambition subverts familial loyalty; and Brutus's wounding of Caesar may be the most telling instance of this.

It seems that a consensus about Brutus will always prove elusive. The more we reflect on these diverse readings, the more it becomes evident that the characterisation clearly exemplifies Shakespeare's sophisticated strategy in this play: to present characters and attitudes ambivalently, involving the audience in unfamiliar and taxing ways.

3. Cassius

In Act 1, scene 2, there occurs a long "seduction sequence", in which Cassius urges Brutus to side with the conspirators against Caesar. Brutus prides himself on being honourable: "I love / The name of honour". Cassius reminds him that his ancestor, Lucius Junius Brutus, had helped to establish the republic by being a leading figure in the expulsion from Rome of Lucius Tarquinius Superbus, last of the Roman kings. The case that Cassius offers against Caesar is that, although he is a mere fallible man, he has become god-like. When Caesar and his train reappear from the Lupercalia, Caesar shrewdly observes to Antony that Cassius, who has a "lean and hungry look", is dangerous, resenting the presence of a greater man. Later, Cassius, alone, gives the game away: he says:

Well, Brutus, thou art noble; yet I see,
Thy honourable mettle may be wrought
From that it is disposed: therefore it is meet
That noble minds keep ever with their likes;
For who so firm that cannot be seduced?

68

Caesar doth bear me hard, but he loves Brutus.
If I were Brutus now, and he were Cassius,
He should not humour me. [1.2]

There Cassius admits that he has sought to seduce the noble Brutus to an ignoble course – a course that Cassius *himself* would not take if he were a favourite of Caesar, as Brutus is. Next, Cassius will deceive Brutus by sending to Brutus those forged letters, purportedly from citizens resentful of Caesar. So, already, the case against Caesar is largely discredited: it stems mainly from Cassius's resentment and envy. Caesar had been shrewd in distrusting him, stating:

Seldom he smiles, and smiles in such a sort
As if he mocked himself and scorned his spirit
That could be moved to smile at any thing.
Such men as he be never at heart's ease
Whiles they behold a greater than themselves,
And therefore are they very dangerous. [1.2]

Furthermore, Cassius, who jeers at Caesar's physical infirmities, is later revealed to have poor eyesight ("My sight was ever thick"). And, like Caesar (and Brutus), Cassius can refer to himself in the third person, as if he were a historic figure: "this very day / Was Cassius born".

During the scene of his quarrel with Brutus (4.2), however, Cassius' complexity is evident: though tainted by corruption, he is horrified by Brutus's denunciation, and eventually, in desperation, offers his life to Brutus. It's a superbly passionate speech: a fine blend of self-pity, exasperation, desperation, frustrated love and anguished emotional blackmail:

Come, Antony, and young Octavius, come,
Revenge yourselves alone on Cassius,
For Cassius is aweary of the world:
Hated by one he loves, braved by his brother,
Checked like a bondman, all his faults observed,
Set in a note-book, learned and conned by rote,
To cast into my teeth. O, I could weep
My spirit from mine eyes! There is my dagger,
And here my naked breast; within, a heart,
Dearer than Pluto's mine, richer than gold:
If that thou be'st a Roman, take it forth.
I, that denied thee gold, will give my heart:
Strike, as thou didst at Caesar; for I know,
When thou didst hate him worst, thou lovedst him
better
Than ever thou lovedst Cassius.

Cassius cannot deny his faults; he can only complain that they are being recited in detail to him by "one he loves": and at "O, I could weep / My spirit from mine eyes!", the exasperation rings truly and intensely. The effect of referring to "Cassius" instead of "I" or "me" is subtle: there is an element of self-pitying self-objectifying: he invokes, so to speak, "the character known to others as Cassius". He offers his breast to the dagger, a form of emotional blackmail (he surely knows that Brutus won't kill him): the gesture is both histrionic and spontaneous, melodramatic yet genuinely dramatic. He sounds passionately sincere, and surely he *is* sincere, at least in these moments; we may well forget the Cassius who prided himself on manipulating and deceiving Brutus. In its contorted but vehement way, there is a genuine passion here, as he invokes the belief that love should transcend or cancel faults. And finally, a bizarre jealousy is revealed, in the allegation that Brutus loved Caesar, whom he killed, more than he ever loved Cassius. Yet again, Caesar, after death, is a divisive force against his foes.

Cassius's impassioned rhetoric proves fully persuasive: Brutus and Cassius are poignantly reconciled. Eventually both will die nobly on the battlefield. Cassius's love and admiration for Brutus become increasingly manifest, overcoming the early envy, and they largely redeem his character. In the famous film directed by Joseph L. Mankiewicz, 1953, John Gielgud, who so often brought finely articulate sensitivity to a characterisation, made this love and admiration poignantly evident. (Indeed, Gielgud received a BAFTA award for that performance as Cassius.) Titinius says to the dead Cassius, "Alas, thou hast miscónstrued everything". But Cassius shares with Brutus and Caesar the capacity to misconstrue. Perhaps the character best able to construe is Antony: in which case, perspicacity is linked to callousness.

According to David Daiches, Cassius is, with Brutus, "the co-hero of the play". He is motivated by envy, and can be duplicitous and crooked – "old Cassius still", says Antony; yet he can be described eventually as "the last of all the Romans". He sees matters in personal terms, and can be highly emotional, as when he swings between anger and grief in that quarrel with Brutus; and he repeatedly makes dramatic gestures, such as exposing himself to thunder and lightning, or threatening to kill himself if the conspiracy is discovered. David Elloway notes that

> the tone of violent jealousy at the end of the quarrel is unmistakable, and suggests that the cynicism with which he had previously contemplated his success in wooing Brutus away from Caesar reflects the spite of a jealous lover as well as the self-satisfaction of a scheming politician, The concern that Cassius expresses on his first approach to Brutus that he is not receiving the "show of love" from him that he "was wont to have" (1.2.34) may be more genuinely felt that might at first appear.

Though calculating and crafty, Cassius, when compared to Antony and Octavius, seems soft-hearted. Within moments of the killing of Caesar, both Brutus and Cassius show a touching concern for Publius, evidently elderly, who is bewildered by the event: they urge him to depart, "Lest that the people, / Rushing on us, should do your age some mischief". It's a fine detail: it shows that although the two conspirators regard their situation as perilous, they are concerned to protect a senator who is not of their party. Cassius's craftiness is surpassed by Shakespeare's, here following an agenda of calculated ambivalence.

Incidentally, some editors magnify Cassius's role. Near the end of Act 2, scene 2, conspirators call on Caesar, to accompany him to the Senate House. Among them is Publius, who is not part of the conspiracy (see 3.1.85-95): he exchanges greetings with Caesar. Cassius is absent. Various editors (for example, those of the 1997 Norton Shakespeare, Stephen Greenblatt and his associates) seek to "improve" Shakespeare by substituting Cassius for

Publius. But it is quite in character for the crafty Cassius to be sometimes "behind the scenes" rather than out in the open.

When editors meddle with Shakespeare, as when they delete Innogen from *Much Ado about Nothing*, or when they change the Dolphin of *Henry V* into the Dauphin, they often make his work more conventional and less interesting.

4. Mark Antony

In 1898 there was a very successful revival of the play by Beerbohm Tree in London. Here Antony, played by Tree, was the dominant character, and the text was trimmed to enhance his dominance. His duplicity was removed, and the proscription scene (Act 4, sc. 1) was deleted. After his climactic funeral oration, parts other than Antony's were reduced. The crowd scenes, spectacular in scale, were superbly effective: 250 performers were employed. (The elaborate sets and Roman costumes were designed by Sir Lawrence Alma-Tadema, the artist renowned for impressive classical subjects.) In 1926, in a London production by Harcourt Williams, Antony was the "undeniable star", being performed by (again) the versatile John Gielgud.

The Antony of Shakespeare's text is a vigorous and complex characterisation. Initially he is presented as a loyal henchman of Caesar; Cassius thinks he may be a dangerous adversary, but Brutus over-rules him, claiming that Antony is merely one "given / To sports, to wildness and much company". (Caesar notes that he "revels long a-nights". Later, Cassius

will mock Antony as "a masker and a reveller".)
Nevertheless, when we first see Antony, he is lightly
clad as a runner at the celebrations. In view of the
emphasis placed on Caesar's physical failings, and
given that Calphurnia, Ligarius and Cassius have
physical impairments, this introduction of Antony as
an athletic figure associated with fertility has some
symbolic force; and Cassius rightly fears that Antony
will prove "a shrewd contriver" who may "annoy us
all" – all the conspirators.

After the assassination, Antony shrewdly sends his
servant to ascertain that he himself may safely
approach the assassins; then Antony appears, and
boldly tells them that he is prepared to die now,
alongside Caesar, all of whose "conquests, glories,
triumphs, spoils" have, seemingly, resulted in this
mere corpse: a Caesar who has been slain by (in
Antony's ironic terms) "the choice and master spirits
of this age". Astutely, Antony manages the perilously
tricky situation. He shakes the bloodstained hands of
the assassins, but reflects on how dismayed Caesar
would be to behold such an act of apparent treachery;
and he makes clear his enduring love for Caesar,
while telling the conspirators that he is willing to be
friends with them if they can prove that Caesar was
dangerous. His love for Caesar is evidently genuine,
and Cassius had previously feared it (2.1.183-4).
Again over-ruling the apprehensive Cassius, Brutus
promises that Antony may indeed give a funeral
oration for Caesar.

That oration, of course, is so brilliantly calculated
and passionately delivered that it turns the crowd
against the conspirators. The critic John Palmer has
suggested that it is precisely because he is given to

"much company" that Antony can establish such a rapport with the crowd, calling them his "gentle friends". His rhetoric having succeeded, Antony then makes the callous (even Iago-ish) comment:

Mischief, thou art afoot,
Take thou what course thou wilt. [3.2]

The immediate outcome includes arson, the flight of Brutus and Cassius, and the savage murder of Cinna the poet. In W. B. Yeats's words: "Things fall apart; the centre cannot hold; / Mere anarchy is loosed upon the world". Coppélia Kahn, a feminist commentator, has claimed that the revenge evoked by Antony "has a feminine character": grief is transmuted into ferocity recalling the Furies of Aeschylus's *Oresteia*. In a recent stage-production (directed by Dominic Dromgoole), Cinna the poet was fiercely and blatantly emasculated by an eager female rioter.

Then Act 4, scene 1, reveals with startling clarity just how ruthless and cynical Antony and Octavius can be. With Lepidus, they prepare a list of enemies to be slain. One is Lepidus's brother; another is Antony's nephew. (Political ambitions become anti-familial.) Then Lepidus is sent for Caesar's will, which evidently will be manipulated by this triumvirate to bring them money: they are financially corrupt. When Lepidus has gone, Antony tells Octavius that he wants Leipidus to be discarded "like to the empty ass", and Octavius agrees. Later, on the eve of the battle of Philippi, Antony with scornful invective reminds Brutus and Cassius of the treacherous nature of their attack on Caesar; though

Antony, as we have seen, is not averse to employing treachery for his own ends. Yet Antony is truly magnanimous to the captured Lucillius:

> Keep this man safe;
> Give him all kindness. I had rather have
> Such men my friends than enemies. [5.4]

After the battle, the victorious Antony pays a generous tribute to the fallen Brutus.

Already in the play, the brief disagreements between Antony and Octavius portend the civil war between them which will be dramatised in *Antony and Cleopatra*. When Octavius in Act 5, sc. 1, contradicts Antony by insisting on leading his army to the right, he says: "I do not cross you; but I *will* do so." There he sounds as imperious as the Julius Caesar who had said "The cause is in my will: I *will* not come". We hear the voice of the future imperial autocrat. Octavius, cold, calculating and assured, is destined for political success: inevitably, and alas. Yet, typically of *Julius Caesar*, even Octavius can sometimes display magnanimity: he promises to give employment to all the men who served his foe, Brutus; and the dead Brutus will be granted "all respect and rites of burial".

In the second tetralogy (*Richard II*, *Henry IV Parts 1 and 2*, and *Henry V*), Shakespeare had involved the audience by setting up numerous comparisons. Who is fitter to rule, Richard or Bolingbroke? Who would be the better heir to the throne, Hotspur or Henry? Whose view of honour is better, Hotspur's (romantic) or Falstaff's (cynical)? As we see, this method of "involvement by comparison" reaches a culmination in *Julius Caesar*, which has no fewer than four candidates for the role of "most important character".

Politicians often seek to impose demeaning stereotypes upon their opponents. Shakespeare in *Julius Caesar* provides an antidote to the widespread political malaise. As we search the characterisations, discovering their ambivalences, we are learning the inadequacy and perils of stereotyping. Shakespeare himself had learnt the lesson: he has here become far more circumspect than the dramatist who once demonised Joan of Arc and Richard III. In *Henry VI, Part 1*, Joan is aided by fiends, to whom she offers her body and soul. In *Richard III*, the physically deformed Richard is "that bottled spider, that foul bunch-backed toad":

Earth gapes, hell burns, fiends roar, saints pray,
To have him suddenly conveyed from hence. [4.4]

But now, in *Julius Caesar*, William Shakespeare revels in contrastingly ambivalent characterisation and ironic plotting.

Julius Caesar: one-man band?

In the play's first scene, the tribunes Flavius and Murellus interrupt the garlanding of Caesar's images. In the second scene, they form part of Caesar's procession. Later in scene 2, Caska says: "Flavius and Murellus, for pulling scarves off Caesar's images, are put to silence." The phrase "put to silence" surely means "put to death": the *Oxford English Dictionary* confirms that.

The implications of Caska's remark are great. Within a very short time, two critics of Caesar's ambition have been identified and (presumably after some very brief summary trial) have been executed. So Caesar has a state apparatus which is alert to sedition and protects him, ruthlessly and efficiently, against it. We are reminded of the obvious: that Caesar cannot govern single-handedly but must have helpers, officials, ministers of justice, civil servants: an extensive supportive apparatus must be in place. Perhaps a glimpse of this is given in the procession of scene 2, which includes Mark Antony, Decius and Cicero.

Yet, for much of the time, the play gives the impression that the government of Caesar is a one-man band: it is Caesar alone wielding power. This effect is created by the fact that the conspirators repeatedly focus their attention on just one man, Caesar himself. The only conspicuous exception comes when Cassius seeks the death of Mark Antony, fearing his loyalty to Caesar. Generally, however, the conspirators, and we in turn, think of Caesar as sole ruler, a lonely autocrat. Caesar's own rhetoric helps to create that impression: he is "constant as the Northern Star", the "one / That unassailable holds on his rank". At the assassination, nobody comes to Caesar's aid. (Plutarch says that those present who were not conspirators were so amazed that they neither moved nor cried out. After the killing, they fled.)

Thus Shakespeare achieves intense dramatic focus, but he does so by rendering almost invisible the customary apparatus of government. The historic Caesar had employed various assistants, notably Oppius and Balbus; and a college of pontiffs helped to administer justice. He greatly increased the number of praetors (magistrates), and he appointed hundreds of new senators. His colonisation programme required numerous administrators, as did his distribution of land to citizens and soldiers.

Of course, if Shakespeare had endeavoured to depict "the customary apparatus of government", the result might have entailed a cluttered stage, an expensive abundance of actors, and a muffling of dramatic clarity. Thomas Carlyle says "The history of the world is but the biography of great men". This is a fallacy, but one which, at first, Shakespeare's treatment of history may appear to support.

On further consideration, though, Shakespeare's treatment of history rather suggests the following maxim: "The history of the world is the product of erring, fallible and myopic men and women, subjects of irony". Sometimes in his plays the operation of divine providence, too, is suggested (as at the finales of *Richard III* and *Henry V*, for example); at other times (as at the end of *Troilus and Cressida* and *King Lear*) divine providence is conspicuously absent.

None of the sources provided a precedent for the peculiarly bleak ending of *King Lear*, in which the death of Cordelia precedes that of the lamenting King. It is relevant that although initially, on his journeys, Lear has a retinue of "a hundred knights and squires", that retinue soon vanishes, so that during the storm on the heath, Lear's only companions are the Fool and Kent. Tragic intensity often tends to isolate the protagonist.

Caesar's ghost and posthumous characterisation

In the play, the spirit of Caesar lives on after the man's assassination. The ghost is active, and helps to bring about the downfall of Brutus and Cassius. The posthumous being modifies the man. The Caesar who lived is thus, in spite of his failings, given the accolade of approval implied by his presence, nature and actions as ghost. Calphurnia had said "When beggars die, there are no comets seen": the supernatural omens surely referred to the great Caesar. He lives on after death, whereas no spectre of Cinna the poet is seen. In *Hamlet*, the provenance of the ghost of Hamlet's father is ambiguous: the Prince himself reflects: "The spirit that I have seen / May be the devil"; but in the pre-Christian world of *Julius Caesar*, there is no suggestion that the spectre that appears to Brutus at Sardis and at Philippi (though an "evil spirit", i.e. an ill-omened spirit for Brutus) is anything other than the ghost of Caesar.

Sceptics may regret this "mystification" of the character, seeing it as superstitious glorification of an autocrat. Recalling other plays, they may relish, instead, the implications of the dying Hamlet's "The rest is silence", or the glum declaration near the end of *King Lear*:

> He hates him,
> That would upon the rack of this tough world
> Stretch him out longer. [5.3]

And such sceptics may think that Prospero told the truth when saying "Our little life / Is rounded with a sleep": no suggestion lurks there of a subsequent awakening. FitzGerald's *The Rubáiyat of Omar Khayyám* may come to mind:

Oh, come with old Khayyám, and leave the Wise
To talk; one thing is certain, that Life flies;
    One thing is certain, and the Rest is Lies;
The Flower that once has blown for ever dies.

Caesar's ghost does, however, indicate a general truth. Posthumous events may modify, retrospectively, a given character. Indeed, the character of Shakespeare himself is not complete until we take account of his posthumous existence. "He was not of an age, but for all time", asserted Ben Jonson; and, as the centuries pass, the element of hyperbole in that assertion diminishes, the hyperbole gradually transmuting itself into an emergent possibility of the factual. As the living Caesar was exalted by his posthumous manifestation, so the living Shakespeare is magnified by his postmortal reputation. Consider these words of sonnets 18 and 55:

So long as men can breathe, or eyes can see,
So long lives this, and this gives life to thee...

And:

Not marble, nor the gilded monuments
Of princes shall outlive this powerful rhyme...

In the course of the accumulating centuries of Shakespeare's fame, the *arrogance* of such declarations becomes progressively transmuted into *authority*. Hyperbole dwindles, being slowly subsumed in fact. Events of this year – revivals of the plays, readings of the poems – are enhancing the character of William Shakespeare, 1564-1616. However infinitesimally, even my words, here and now, are changing him, there and then: rendering him more magisterial. Let us hospitably admit such time-defying transformations. They nurture hope. Something that we make today (whether an essay, a poem, a painting or a table) may have its value increased by events that happen in the future.

Some characterisations have no foreseeable termini. Therein lies a warning for literary critics and for biographers.

Chapter 3: *Julius Caesar* in Shakespeare's time

When *Julius Caesar* was first acted, how did it seem?

On 21 September 1599 a Swiss tourist, Thomas Platter, visiting London, saw a production of *Julius Caesar* at a Bankside theatre with a thatched roof. It is virtually certain that this was Shakespeare's *Julius Caesar* at the newly-opened Globe Theatre. A historic play about a great leader who ruled so much of the known world would have been an appropriate choice for the opening of a theatre bearing that name and the motto *"Totus mundus agit histrionem"* (translated loosely: "All the world's a stage."). The role of Caesar may have been played by Shakespeare, and that of Brutus by Richard Burbage, the company's leading actor.

Platter made notes in German, which, in the translation by Ernest Schanzer, read thus:

On the 21st of September, after dinner, at about two o'clock, I went with my party across the water; in the straw-thatched house we saw the tragedy of the first Emperor Julius Caesar, very pleasingly performed, with approximately fifteen characters; at the end of the play they danced together admirably and exceedingly gracefully, according to their custom, two in each group dressed in men's and two in women's apparel...

Thus every day around two o'clock in the afternoon in the city of London two and sometimes even three plays are performed at different places, in order to make people merry... The places are built in such a way that they act on a raised scaffold, and everyone can well see everything. However, there are separate galleries and places, where one sits more pleasantly and better, therefore also pays more. For he who remains standing below pays only one English penny, but if he wants to sit he is let in at another door, where he gives a further penny; but if he desires to sit on cushions in the pleasantest place, where he not only sees everything but can also be seen, then he pays at a further door another English penny. And during the play food and drink is carried around, among the people, so that one can also refresh oneself for one's money.

The play-actors are dressed most exquisitely and elegantly, because of the custom in England that when men of rank or knights die they give and bequeath almost their finest apparel to their servants, who, since it does not befit them, do not wear such garments, but afterwards let the play-actors buy them for a few pence...

Several features of Platter's report are notable. First: he refers to the play as "the tragedy of the first Emperor" ("*die Tragedy vom ersten Keyser*"). The title "Emperor" implies that, in Platter's view, the play's Caesar had *already* ended the era of republican Rome. In registering this, Platter is shrewder than Brutus.

Secondly, Platter says that as a coda to the play there was graceful dancing by the actors, in each group "two... dressed in men's and two in women's apparel". The tragic tradition is believed to derive from fertility rituals and, in ancient Greece, from the worship of Dionysus, a "dying and rising" god. After being torn apart by Titans, Dionysus (god of wine and

85

ecstasy) was reborn and lived immortally: he is associated with the natural cycle, whereby vegetation appears to die in winter but is reborn in the spring. The vine, after its apparent death, is regenerated. The god's death was mourned, but in his resurrection were grounds for celebration. There's a link with Decius's interpretation of the strange dream featuring Caesar's bleeding statue: he interprets it to mean that from Caesar's blood Romans will derive nourishment and sustenance.

"Tragoidia", Greek for "tragedy", originally meant "goat-song": a song in fertility-rituals, celebrating the goat, for goats are notoriously randy. The Roman Lupercalia, dramatised in Act 1, sc. 2, was, as we have noted, a fertility festival: barren women were supposedly rendered fertile, and goats were sacrificed. As we have also noted, in Athens of the 5th century B.C., at the drama festivals where the priest of Dionysus had an honoured place, it was customary for each trilogy of tragic plays to be followed by a comic satyr play: after the grim and sombre, the comic and buffoonish. In the dancing witnessed by Platter, we may infer a continuation of the ancient notion that, after death, life should be happily reasserted. Shakespeare's late romances (*Pericles, Cymbeline, The Winter's Tale and The Tempest*) will incorporate tragic material – suffering and death – within a structure which finally entails a restorative resolution. Indeed, those late romances seen as a group, following such intense tragic works as *Hamlet, Othello, King Lear* and *Macbeth*, can be regarded as the post-tragic restorative affirmation.

Platter's remarks on the pricing-structure are a reminder of the social range of the Globe's audience of 1,500. One penny was all that an apprentice or a workman needed for entry, while three pence (and more) would buy admission for a well-to-do person who wished to see and "also be seen". This has a bearing on the content of the play *Julius Caesar* itself. One can imagine groundlings (in the cheapest standing places near the apron stage) sympathising with the cheeky cobbler in the first scene. Some well-to-do patrons, loyal to Queen Elizabeth, might well sympathise with Caesar; others (friends of Essex and Southampton, perhaps) might sympathise with the conspirators. And many in the audience would experience divided allegiances. Meanwhile, Shakespeare, a shareholder in the Globe, would collect his percentage of the box-office receipts.

Platter says that food and drink were sold and distributed during the actual performance. In the 20th century, the Marxist dramatist Bertolt Brecht praised the theatre of Shakespeare's day for being "earthy, profane and lacking in magic", but added that "People were supposed to use their imaginations" – presumably to provide that missing magic. In the circumstances described by Platter, the subtleties of Elizabethan drama become the more remarkable. We can imagine the clinking of tankards and the cracking of hazel-nuts during a tense soliloquy; and we may be reminded of modern jazz sessions at which subtly meditative playing by George Shearing, Stan Tracey or Dave Drake has been accompanied by the clattering of glasses and the chattering of patrons at the back of the club. When Hamlet complains that "the groundlings... for the most part are capable of nothing but inexplicable dumb-shows and noise", he is, nevertheless, standing within a few feet of numerous groundlings whose appreciation of *Hamlet* helped to make it an evident commercial and critical success.

Platter's remark on the recycling of noblemen's clothing suggests that in *Julius Caesar*, the actors might be more likely to be costumed in contemporary English outfits than in authentic Roman outfits. In practice, a chronological mixture of outfits prevailed, as is indicated by a contemporaneous picture (a drawing by Henry Peacham) of characters in *Titus Andronicus*. There two figures (perhaps Titus's sons, probably attendant soldiers) wear Elizabethan costume; the other men are wearing more-or-less classical attire; and the flowing regal robe worn by Tamora, Queen of the Goths, is, if not classical, at least un-Elizabethan. And such a mixture would signal visually the interaction of past and present in the theatrical experience: the combination of the historic and the topical. Far from raising cries of "anachronism!", it would facilitate the interpretation of the play about the past as a commentary on the present.

What was the topical relevance of *Julius Caesar*?

Certainly, dramas set in the historic past could be a way – a rather risky way – of commenting on contemporaneous politics.

Fulke Greville wrote a tragedy about Antony and Cleopatra, but burnt it, fearing that the eponymous characters would be associated with the Earl of Essex and Queen Elizabeth. On 8 February 1601, that Earl of Essex, accompanied by the Earl of Southampton (Shakespeare's patron), led an insurrection against Elizabeth. The insurrection failed; Essex was executed; Southampton was sentenced to death, but the sentence was commuted to one of life imprisonment. On the eve of the uprising, as we have noted, Essex's supporters paid Shakespeare's company to stage a performance of *Richard II*, evidently thinking that this play about a successful revolt against a monarch would hearten the insurrectionists. "I am Richard II[:] know ye not that?", declared the indignant Queen.

Julius Caesar, too, would have borne contemporaneous relevance. In 1570, in the papal bull "*Regnans in Excelsis*" ("Reigning high above"), Pope Pius V had made evident to Catholics that Elizabeth, declared a heretical usurper of the throne, was a legitimate target for assassination. Numerous assassination attempts ensued. In 1571 there was the Ridolfi plot; in 1583 the Throgmorton plot; and in 1586 the Babington plot. The Queen told the French Ambassador in 1583, "There are more than two hundred men of all ages who, at the instigation of the

Jesuits, conspire to kill me." By 1599, when *Julius Caesar* was first performed, Elizabeth was ageing and ailing, and there were worries about the succession, as the childless "Virgin Queen" had no direct heir. The possibility of a revolt against Elizabeth was real, as the Earl of Essex was to prove within seventeen months of the performance described by Thomas Platter. Indeed, when depicting Brutus, Shakespeare was perhaps "speaking up for the embattled Essex", speculates Anthony Holden. (But, if so, Shakespeare, as we have seen, was surely speaking with forked tongue.)

Colin Burrow says:

The creation of that ancient world [by Shakespeare] derived from an extraordinary convergence between highly fashionable historical sources and the anxieties of the present moment. It's this fusion of the old and the new which makes the play continue to be electrifying.

What was *Julius Caesar*'s place in Shakespeare's career?

Roland Barthes, in the deftly ironic essay "La Mort de l'auteur" ("The Death of the Author", 1968) satirised the old-fashioned notion that the author of a literary work should be ignored by critics of that work. Some naive readers took this satiric piece literally; but, as J. C. Carlier pointed out, the irony was made evident by the fact that Barthes signed the essay and claimed copyright for it. In any case, readers who took the piece literally were committed to the view that the meaning of a work was constructed by the reader; in which case, Carlier's interpretation remained irrefutable.

Hence the relevance of Colin Burrow's article "Very New and Very Old" (*Around the Globe*, Summer 2014), in which Burrow explains that *Julius Caesar* emerged at a critical time in Shakespeare's career. It was the first of his plays to be performed at the newly-constructed Globe Theatre, and Shakespeare had made a big and risky investment, buying a one-tenth share of the profits. "June 1599, when *Julius Caesar* probably first opened, would make or break him." Burrow continues:

Shakespeare seems to be on his best behaviour. *Julius Caesar* has no major comic parts, although Shakespeare's most popular character by this date was Sir John Falstaff... It contains long and ostentatiously crafted speeches, and dramatizes a rhetorical competition between Antony and Brutus... Brutus and Antony were regarded as the finest orators of their generation, so it was extraordinarily bold to recreate their rhetorical skill onstage. Shakespeare used the opening of the Globe theatre to outdo himself.

The place of *Julius Caesar* within Shakespeare's professional and financial life may also explain why its finest scenes are so full of anxiety.

A mood of anxiety indeed courses through numerous scenes, though the tensions of the plot may sufficiently account for them. (But perhaps anxiety led the author to choose that plot-material.) As for the rhetorical features: the great scene of rival oratory (3.2) would have exploited superbly the Globe's apron stage, with the audience on its three sides. In theatres today, that scene can still work stirringly in a way that cannot be replicated in the cinema, which separates the audience impermeably from the crowd on the screen. The present Globe Theatre in London facilitates lively interaction between the orators on stage and the responsive audience around it, as was well illustrated when Luke Thompson, with impassioned rhetoric, played Mark Antony there in 2014.

If Shakespeare did experience financial anxiety, it would have been allayed by his increasing commercial success over the years: his gamble at the Globe paid handsomely. In 1599, however, he may well have experienced political anxiety. In that year "the Bishops' Ban" on satires and epigrams had resulted in the public burning of books by Marston, Middleton and others. In May, all copies of John Hayward's account of Henry IV were called in and burnt. "It is perhaps little wonder that *Julius Caesar* is a nervous play", comments Andrew Hadfield. We recall that the play opens with a double action of censorship: Flavius and Murellus strip the trophies from busts of Caesar, but in turn are silenced.

We know from his sonnets that Shakespeare was bitterly aware of censorship in England: sonnet 66 deplores "art made tongue-tied by authority, / And folly (doctor-like) controlling skill". A few years after *Julius Caesar* was first performed, Ben Jonson's *Sejanus* was staged, unsuccessfully; Shakespeare was one of the actors. In that Roman play, Cremutius Cordus, a historian, is charged with sedition, because his writings praise Brutus and Cassius as worthy republicans. We are not told his fate, but his books are burnt. (In reality, the historic Cremutius Cordus was forced to commit suicide.) Ben Jonson later said that he himself had been summoned before the Privy Council and charged with "Popery and treason" on the basis of his play. One reason may have been that Sejanus is a corrupt and ruthless royal favourite, and King James's attachment to a sequence of male favourites (some sharing his bed) was well known. On that occasion, Jonson seems to have escaped punishment.

Compared with *Julius Caesar*, *Sejanus* seems slow and pedantic; its moral emphases are protracted and obvious, and as a whole it is oddly un-dramatic: the overthrow of Sejanus himself by Macro is easily if lengthily achieved. *Julius Caesar* is not only more subtle, by virtue of the ambiguous characterisation; it is also far more dramatic, vividly so; it is interlaced with ironies; and, from time to time, it radiates a warmth of intimate "human interest" that is lacking from Jonson's rather Marlovian depiction of the arrogant over-reacher. Shakespeare's awareness of the risk of censorship and of official disapproval may have helped to nourish those ambivalent features which are so prominent in *Julius Caesar.*

Censorship, conventionally regarded as oppressive and repressive, can have positive creative consequences.

Anachronisms: do they matter?

Professor John Sutherland says:

The shooting of a vastly expensive crowd scene in one of Cecil B. de Mille's biblical epics was (supposedly) ruined when it was seen during the "rushes" that one of the bare-armed centurions was still wearing his wrist-watch.

Shakespeare's *Julius Caesar* offers a fine hunting-ground for pursuers of anachronisms. At night a clock strikes three (2.1.292), even though, in Italy, bells were first cast in Naples around the 8th century A.D.; and mechanical clocks were not invented until the 12th or 13th century. Shakespeare's Romans anachronistically wear "sweaty night-caps" (1.2.243). Brutus is termed "Caesar's angel" (3.2.180), and Cassius cites Satan ("th'eternal Devil", 1.2.160): premature Christian imagery. A book has its leaf turned down (4.2.323), but there were no books in Rome, only inscribed slates and scrolls. The reference to "chimney-tops" (1.1.39) evokes Elizabethan London rather than ancient Rome. There is no anachronism in the reference to Roman hats at 2.1.73, as ancient Romans did wear various forms of hat. Even the reference to "doublets" (jackets, 1.2.62) is compatible with some kinds of Roman clothing. The mention of actors' expressions and styles (2.1.225-7) is passably compatible with the fact that Roman actors wore full masks and half-masks. As we have noted, the Peacham drawing of a scene from *Titus Andronicus* depicts costumes of diverse eras, ranging from ancient to Elizabethan.

In *Julius Caesar*, as we already tolerate the conventions that these ancient Romans speak Elizabethan English and are fluent in blank verse, it should not be difficult to accommodate anachronisms. These may even lend an occasional surrealistic spicing to the largely realistic mode. Between you and me: Shakespeare's blunders make him more likeable – more like *us*. In any case, even William Golding's masterpiece, *Lord of the Flies*, has a plot dependent on impossibility: the myopic Piggy's spectacles are used to make fire, essential to the story; but such convex lenses would, in reality, never focus the sun's rays sufficiently. Great literary works can, with the readers' co-operation, absorb bizarre errors. "To err is human; to forgive, divine."

Chapter 4: Analyses

Is Shakespeare's Roman world really "flatter"?

Dr Johnson remarked that in *Julius Caesar*, Shakespeare's "adherence to the real story, and to *Roman* manners, seems to have impeded the natural vigour of his genius". A recent critic, Adrian Poole, considering Shakespeare's depiction of Rome, says:

All Shakespeare's history plays, English and Roman, address moments of massive turbulence in the worlds they represent. But there is a much stronger vertical axis in the English plays... To the English histories the concept of monarchy is essential, and along with it go a whole set of beliefs about the relations between masters and servants, nobles and commoners, and indeed husbands and wives. All these are largely though not wholly absent from "Rome". So too are beliefs in heaven up there and hell down there. In all kinds of ways the world is *flatter* in Rome than it is in "this sceptered isle".

Ancient Rome is the setting – or *a* setting – of several works by Shakespeare: *The Rape of Lucrece*, *Titus Andronicus*, *Julius Caesar*, *Antony and Cleopatra*, *Coriolanus* and *Cymbeline*. Though these works differ greatly from each other, if we discount the anomalous *Cymbeline* we soon see a consistency in Shakespeare's concepts of Rome and *romanitas* (Roman-ness). He associates Rome with patriotism, civic responsibility, public debate, forensic eloquence, and characters who exhibit a proud sense of their own worth and dignity: "honour" and "nobility" are ethical key-terms. (Of course, as Arthur Humphreys has noted, "Shakespeare's Romans, however concerned to be rational, are human enough to use rationality as a mask for assumption".)

Leading Romans seek to maintain their dignified public personae. Repeatedly, as we have seen, they refer to themselves in the third person, as if creating a public self which is larger and more imposing than the mere private self; or, if they use the first person, they still promote the larger-than-life as the true self. Caesar says: "Danger knows full well / That Caesar is more dangerous than he"; and "I rather tell thee what is to be feared, / Than what I fear; for always I am Caesar." Other characters explicitly offer ideal images of themselves: the qualities expected of a Brutus, a Cassius or even a Caska. They parade moral austerity and earnestness. Sometimes they may sacrifice family members rather than undergo loss of prestige. In *Titus Andronicus*, "What, villain boy, / Barr'st me my way in Rome?", cries an enraged Titus before slaying one of his own sons. They exhibit stoical constancy, being prepared to suffer without complaint; and, if necessary, they are prepared to commit suicide ("the high Roman fashion") rather than undergo loss of honour in defeat and humiliation. Titus's brother and son, Marcus and Lucius, say that they will kill themselves if the Roman people disapprove of their conduct. Lucrece, having been raped, commits suicide. Brutus declares: "I love / The name of honour more than I fear death." Brutus and Cassius, when defeated, choose to die.

(Although Rome is the location of political intrigue and treachery, Rome requires and elicits loyalty.)

Thus Shakespeare's Rome has earnest, austere and grave features. We see what is missing if we recall the Egyptian scenes of *Antony and Cleopatra*. There, Egypt connotes sexual indulgence, heady pleasure, festivity, drunkenness, decadence, sensuality, fertility, colourful spectacle, heat, and Nile's fertile mud. Consider Enobarbus's description (in Act 2, sc. 2) of Cleopatra's arrival on the river:

> The barge she sat in, like a burnished throne,
> Burnt on the water: the poop was beaten gold;
> Purple the sails, and so perfumèd that
> The winds were love-sick with them; the oars were
> silver,
> Which to the tune of flutes kept stroke, and made
> The water which they beat to follow faster,
> As amorous of their strokes. For her own person,
> It beggared all description. She did lie,
> In her pavilion, cloth of gold, of tissue,
> O'erpicturing that Venus where we see
> The fancy out-work nature.

It's a vision of radiant erotic opulence. The Rome of *Julius Caesar* is relatively monochrome, the Egypt of *Antony and Cleopatra* is richly coloured; Rome resembles the rational super-ego, Egypt the sensual id. Antony, drawn to Egypt ("i'th'East my pleasure lies") will be defeated politically by the austere Octavius; but in terms of ontological plenitude – sheer amplitude of being, of rich selfhood – Antony and Cleopatra eclipse Octavius. Octavia, Antony's wife, being chastely virtuous, is morally superior to

Cleopatra; but, as a seductive phenomenon, Cleopatra with her "infinite variety", making hungry "where most she satisfies", eclipses Octavia. Compared with the sensuous metaphoric richness of *Antony and Cleopatra*, *Julius Caesar*'s poetry is relatively austere: appropriate to Shakespeare's Rome, which gives prominence to rational control and apparently logical rhetoric. The lucidity of utterance is often achieved, we see, by exclusion: by some suppression of Shakespeare's facility for metaphoric profusion. Repeatedly, emotions are canalised into persuasive discourse.

Again, if you compare the Rome of *Julius Caesar* with the England of *Henry IV*, you see what is missing: this Rome lacks the rumbustious tavern-world of England, and all the anarchic festivity that goes with it. (As the Roman tribunes silence the cheeky cobbler, Shakespeare curbs his own comic exuberance.) England is also a land of agriculture: we are reminded of the seasonal cycle, of the work of the countryside with its wheat-fields and orchards, and of the resultant food on the table. (Seek imagery of food in *Julius Caesar*, and you find Brutus's chilling exhortation to the conspirators, "Let's carve him as a dish fit for the gods".) Hal, soon to be Henry V, has to cope with the massive irreverence and subversive comedy of Falstaff: the official political world is challenged again and again by amoral humour and gusto. (Falstaff, declaring "What is honour? A word... Air", might wreak havoc in Shakespeare's Rome.) Furthermore, the society of *Henry IV* is a Christian society. Political values exist in an uneasy amalgam with Christian values, and Shakespeare is astute in showing how they may run into conflict. Politically,

Bolingbroke is shrewder than Richard, the monarch he overthrows; but Richard, for all his faults, is "The Lord's anointed": he bears the sanctity of a rightful monarch, consecrated: God's deputy on earth; so that the killing of Richard is not only a political act; it is an act of religious sacrilege, and Bolingbroke never loses the ensuing guilt. Henry V will inherit that guilt, and will try to square the circle of being a Christian yet martial monarch. Thus central figures in the English history plays are subject to multiple moral scansion: scansion of the geniality of their humanity, accentuated by voices from the tavern world; scansion of their capacity for mercy and charity, accentuated by echoes of Christian doctrine and biblical lore.

In *Julius Caesar*, Shakespeare retains the supernatural features cited by Plutarch; but they have a very limited ethical basis: they indicate that the assassination is a dire event which will unleash much bloodshed, and they vindicate Caesar, who is given posthumous power to rebuke Brutus. These features lack the scale and the moral range of the Christian ideology.

So Shakespeare's Rome has an ethical thinness, in contrast to the world of the English history plays. But this restriction entails some dramatic strengths, too. For Shakespeare, when using a more limited ethical palette, can offer an elegantly lucid forensic analysis of the political world, and of the ways in which power corrupts and the quest for power may entail a diminution of inner humanity. It's like a meticulously controlled experiment. *Julius Caesar* can serve as an economical, lucid, vivid and memorable dramatisation of the political, and of the passions that political views evoke. It still works; it's still valid.

The recurrent ironic patterning of defeated striving will not be complete until the end of *Antony and Cleopatra*. From that viewpoint, looking back, we see how the ambitions of the great Julius Caesar ended in his gory murder before the statue of his defeated rival, Pompey; but those who killed him, hoping to restore republicanism, in turn die, having helped to bring about the rule of an absolute emperor, Octavius. Antony, who seemed so ruthlessly proficient in *Julius Caesar*, meets, in *Antony and Cleopatra*, a botched death, redeemed by Cleopatra's eloquence.

The main characters in *Julius Caesar* are highly conscious of the need to perform well in public. Rome with its forum is a place of public oratory and debate. The characters, addressing the Roman populace, resemble actors performing in the theatre, and sometimes the theatrical analogy becomes explicit. This play about politics exhibits politics as theatre. As we in the theatre see the audience on stage responding to political rhetoric, we are made aware of the analogies between politics and theatre, and between politicians and actors.

One notable characteristic of Shakespeare's Roman characters is the intense linkage of loyalty and love. Wives prove their love by demonstrating their loyalty; and repeatedly men offer other men the assurance of loyalty intensified by love. In the play, the word "love" and its variants appear 56 times, observes David Daniell; and G. Wilson Knight noted:

There is love expressed or suggested between Brutus and Cassius, Brutus and Caesar, and Antony and Caesar; Brutus and Portia, Brutus and Volumnius, Brutus and Lucius;

Caesar and Decius, Cassius and Lucius Pella, Cassius and Titinius; Ligarius and Brutus, Artemidorus and Caesar.

To that list, we can surely add Calphurnia and Caesar, for Calphurnia is so anxious to save Caesar from peril that she kneels to implore him, as Portia had knelt before Brutus: an ironic likeness which may make us reflect that privately Caesar is not so different from the man who will assail him.

Sometimes, the declarations of love do not inhibit acts of deception or treachery: Cassius will deceive Brutus (by forging persuasive letters), and, of course, Brutus will stab Caesar. But the general effect of these repeated declarations of love is to generate the sense of Rome as a location where loyalty is so highly valued that it entails emotionally-intensifying declarations. Only in Cassius's attitude to Brutus does the love expressed approach the homo-erotic; and stage-productions may emphasise this, although, in the Folio text, it's not a close approach. Wayne Rebhorn points out, however, that in the essay "Of Love", by Shakespeare's near-contemporary Sir William Cornwallis the Younger (1579-1613),

love is defined as a uniting of affections whose primary and ideal – most "celestial" – form involves the agreement of man and man, whereas the relationship of man and woman is secondary and defective because lust affects it too strongly.

These words bring to mind not only Cassius's relationship with Brutus but also the relationships described in Shakespeare's *Sonnets*, in which the poet, infatuated with the dark lady, describes her as "the bay where all men ride" and "this false plague".

In one respect, the Rome of *Julius Caesar* is a highly paradoxical location. Here Shakespeare has heightened a paradox described in Plutarch's pages. Rome is a place of high civilisation, distinguished by forensic reasoning: major characters display and admire the capacity for rational analysis. "The play possesses the surface clarity of polished marble", says Vivien Thomas. Yet this Rome, seemingly the location of reason *par excellence*, is infiltrated and beset by the supernatural, the irrational, the superstitious and the weird. At the Lupercalia, the fertility-festival, Caesar wants Calphurnia to be struck by the running Antony, in the hope that the blow will render her fertile. Augurers search the entrails of a sacrificed creature in order to advise Caesar. Furthermore, a tempest drops fire; a slave's hand burns yet remains unscorched; at the Capitol a lion stares at Caska; another lion whelps in the streets; graves open and release the dead; men on fire are reported to be walking through the city; fiery warriors battle in the clouds, so that blood drizzles down upon the Capitol; ghosts "shriek and squeal"; an owl hoots at noon; and Brutus at night can read by the light of meteors "whizzing in the air" (here audiences often titter incredulously).

Most of these bizarre and diversely-interpreted occurrences give the impression that the actual or intended actions of men are of so important and terrible a kind that they are provoking supernatural responses representing the unnatural, violent and dangerous. They also suggest "the return of the repressed": the irrational and occult forces which civilisation seeks to transcend are here making an angry comeback.

After the assassination, the only supernatural events are the appearance of Caesar as an avenging spirit, and, in Cassius's partly-credulous view, the arrival of ominous "ravens, crows and kites". Predominantly now, the violence is being enacted not in weird visions but in combat between men. Eldritch nightmare is superseded by violent reality.

While Roman rationality has been challenged by the Roman supernatural, Roman orderliness is challenged by the crowd, which, when inflamed by oratory, can rampage chaotically through the streets. The more the main characters display their powers of reasoning, the more we are aware of the passions which they evoke and which move them. The lofty rhetoric of the conspirators is answered by the "poor dumb mouths" of Caesar's wounds. To such idealistic (and tautological) slogans as "Liberty! Freedom! Tyranny is dead!" and "Liberty, freedom and enfranchisement!" and "Peace, freedom and liberty!", the mocking counterpoint is the recurrent imagery of copious bloodshed – from the apparitions, from Portia's wound, from the gushing "statua" of Caesar, from Caesar's many wounds, and eventually from Cassius and Brutus.

The high civilisation of Rome is beleaguered by the threat of chaos from the supernatural, from the populace, and from the lethal lust for power. This, a pervasive irony, is the major paradox of *Julius Caesar*, and the source of so much of the play's dramatic vitality.

Three key scenes

1. Cassius's prophecy: how is it fulfilled?

Julius Caesar is rich in ironies, conceptual and political. They become incisively intense in Act 3, scene 1, when Cassius says to his fellows after they have slain Caesar:

> Stoop, then, and wash. How many ages hence
> Shall this our lofty scene be acted over,
> In states unborn, and accents yet unknown?

The prior context of this speech is that the conspirators have repeatedly stabbed Caesar, who has displayed courage and dignity in his death. Some moments of confusion follow: a mixture of elation, tension, uncertainty and improvised planning. Then, in response to Caska's remark that an early death saves one from years of apprehension, Brutus says:

> Grant that, and then is death a benefit:
> So are we Caesar's friends, that have abridged
> His time of fearing death. Stoop, Romans, stoop,
> And let us bathe our hands in Caesar's blood
> Up to the elbows, and besmear our swords;
> Then walk we forth, even to the market-place,
> And waving our red weapons o'er our heads,
> Let's all cry, "Peace, freedom and liberty!"

Here Cassius makes that quoted prophecy about the "lofty scene", and Brutus caps it by asking

How many times shall Caesar bleed in sport,
That now on Pompey's basis lies along,
No worthier than the dust?

When Cassius says, "Stoop, then, and wash", he is
endorsing Brutus's plan to ritualise the murder. By
deliberately smearing themselves in blood, the
conspirators symbolise their readiness to share
responsibility for the assassination and to declare
publicly their commitment. They seek to tidy by ritual
and rhetoric a rather messy killing. But their ritual
spreads the mess. This washing is no cleansing but a
pollution.

This symbolic ceremony was devised by
Shakespeare. Plutarch's *Lives* says only that the
assassins became smeared with blood in the general
mêlée, in which some of them accidentally wounded
each other. Shakespeare confers on the historic event
the conspirators' deliberate endeavour to dignify it by
ritual.

In turn, however, the context mocks their attempt.
In the theatre, their excited rhetoric is mocked by the
stillness of Caesar's corpse, which lies beside them;
and their smearing of swords and arms ("up to the
elbows") in blood resembles an unholy sacrament or
profane baptism, an open gory acknowledgement of
murderous guilt which challenges their idealistic
words. The proposed cry, "Peace, freedom and
liberty!", inevitably seems ironic when uttered by
men who flaunt the blood of a ruler whose "freedom
and liberty" have been so belligerently curtailed.

Consider again the resonance of those words about
the "lofty scene" being re-enacted "in states unborn,
and accents yet unknown". In the first place, the

words are strikingly self-validating. A historic event, the actual killing of Julius Caesar in ancient Rome, is indeed being re-enacted: re-enacted, in Shakespeare's day, in Elizabethan England, a state "unborn" in Caesar's time, and proclaimed in "accents yet unknown" – Elizabethan English, not classical Latin. The fictional killers are making a speculative prophecy which is automatically fulfilled by the very fact of the play's performance. The scene on stage evokes a past in which speakers herald that very scene on stage. Fact and fiction, reality and performance, past and present, blur into each other; we participate in paradoxical time-travel.

In modern times, the prophecy is *emphatically* fulfilled, since the states in which stage-productions are seen may include those "unborn" (from the colonisers' if not the indigenes' viewpoint) in Shakespeare's day, e.g. Canada or Australia; and the "accents yet unknown" may include American accents, or, if the play is being performed in translation, German, Russian, Japanese, or even Swahili (in *Juliasi Kaizari*), for example. The prophecy, then, was not only curiously self-validating in the Elizabethan period; it has gained even greater validation as Shakespeare's works have travelled on through time and around the world.

Cassius's phrase "lofty scene" has many ironies. The assassination of a ruler as powerful as Caesar is indeed the stuff of great tragedies, as Cassius knows. But his phrase is part of a deliberate attempt to vindicate a murder by endowing it with noble significance. Audiences have just seen one man – an ageing, half-deaf man – being ambushed, goaded, and slaughtered by numerous conspirators. The staging requires a copious blood-flow, to be true to the text. It looks like a messy, nasty death; and, quite probably, our imaginative sympathies are extended to Caesar, the outnumbered but plucky underdog in the situation, while our imaginative antipathy is likely to be directed against the assassins.

We may recall the affability with which Caesar had greeted them when they called to escort him. While offering general thanks for their "pains and courtesy", to Caius Ligarius he had said "Caesar was ne'er so much your enemy / As that same ague which hath made you lean", and he had invited Trebonius to an hour's talk later, concluding:

Good friends, go in and taste some wine with me,
And we, like friends, will straightway go together.
[2.2]

So, when Brutus, after the killing, offers the argument that the slayers have actually done their victim a favour by "abridg[ing] his time of fearing death", we may smile sceptically at this rationalisation of a particularly treacherous murder. Furthermore, though the action is "lofty" in having historical importance, it is obviously not "lofty" in the sense of having noble dignity. Certainly Caesar will, as Brutus foretold, "die in sport", as entertainment, on many occasions. In *Hamlet*, Polonius offers confirmation when he remarks, "I did enact Julius Caesar. I was killed i'th'Capitol: Brutus killed me", and Polonius will, ironically, be assassinated himself soon after making this remark. The large irony unrecognised by Brutus and Cassius is that when their action is re-enacted in the theatre, they may well be seen at that point as villains, or as naively misguided political activists, rather than as heroes. Of course, responses will vary, as will the actors' and directors' interpretations; but it is hard to acclaim the killers of an unarmed victim, and the dead Caesar's silence is at least as eloquent as Cassius's rhetoric.

Whenever the scene is performed, says Cassius,

> So often shall the knot of us be called
> "The men that gave their country liberty". [3.1]

"Liberty" for whom? Not for the women and slaves, certainly. What the play shows, of course, is that, far from inaugurating an era of liberty, the conspirators inaugurate an era of bloody conflict. Brutus and Cassius are obliged to go into battle, and are defeated by the alliance of Mark Antony, Octavius and Lepidus, and by their own misjudgements.

Audiences readily sympathise with underdogs, and Brutus and Cassius become more sympathetic as they face defeat. We know from *Antony and Cleopatra* that the victorious triumvirate will soon fall to dissension, and eventually Antony will die defeated by the ruthless and calculating Octavius. Before the end of *Julius Caesar*, there are portents of the dissension to come: in Act 4, scene 1, Antony persuades Octavius to conspire with him against Lepidus; and in Act 5, scene 1, Octavius insists on over-ruling Antony's tactical judgement.

So, politically, the paraphrasable message of *Julius Caesar* may seem much the same as that of *Hamlet* or *Macbeth*: it is an apparently conservative message. People who conspire to depose or kill the established ruler may succeed for a while, but they may be burdened with guilt, they will provoke increasing disorder, and they themselves may well be defeated and killed in turn. Nevertheless, as we have seen, there is a long theatrical tradition of depicting Brutus as the noble defender of liberty.

A final dimension of irony besets Cassius's question, "How many ages hence / Shall this our lofty scene be acted over...?". Brutus takes the words to mean that in future, the assassination of Caesar will be performed on stage. There is, of course, another meaning, of which Cassius may be unaware. The "lofty scene", the present great performance, may be "acted over" not on stage but in stark reality. Brutus and Cassius will have provided precedent for subsequent bloody deeds, undertaken perhaps in the names of "Peace, freedom and liberty", which, like their own misconceived venture, will result not in a new Golden Age but in further bloodshed, fresh disillusionment, and the restoration of Caesarism – of autocracy in one form or another.

Modern audiences may recall that the English Civil War, in which Charles I was executed, resulted in the autocratic "Protectorate" of Oliver Cromwell. They may recall that the French Revolution, with its watchwords of "*Liberté, Égalité, Fraternité*", resulted in the death of a king and the carnage inflicted by the guillotine, the invasion of republican Switzerland by the revolutionary army, and eventually in the emergence of Napoleon as autocratic emperor. Or they may recall that the communistic ideals of the Russian revolutionaries were mocked by the subsequent triumph of the dictatorial Joseph Stalin.

As for political assassinations, they have generally done more harm than good. Certainly, we may wish that the bomb-plot against Hitler in 1944 had succeeded. But the assassination of the Nazi leader, Reinhard Heydrich, in Prague in 1942 resulted in hideous large-scale reprisals against the civilian population: 13,000 people were arrested and about five thousand died, sometimes after torture; the village of Lidice was razed. The killing of Franz Ferdinand, the Austrian Grand Duke, by a Serb in 1914 precipitated a war in which millions died. The slayings of Mahatma Gandhi in 1948, President J. F. Kennedy in 1963, Martin Luther King Junior in 1968 and Lord Mountbatten in 1979 were widely regarded as lamentable. As we have noted, in 2011 the assassination of the Libyan dictator, Muammar Gaddafi, inaugurated not a flourishing democracy but a civil war which ravaged Libya for years.

For us, today, therefore, there is a peculiarly grim irony in the sanguine hopes of Brutus and Cassius that their deeds will be re-enacted "in states unborn, and accents yet unknown". Shakespeare's bloodstained conspirators have indeed proven truer prophets than they (or even their author, perhaps) could ever have foreseen. History, alas, has repeatedly provided ironic fulfilment of the conspirators' sanguine prediction.

2. The rival orations: how do they work?

In Act 3, sc. 2, Brutus's oration at the Forum is in prose, and it is highly patterned: the rhetorical artifice is conspicuous. Clearly, Brutus has studied the art of oratory. A favoured device is the repetition of grammatical units. Consider, for instance:

Hear me for my cause, and be silent, that ye may hear. Believe me for mine honour, and have respect to mine honour, that ye may believe. Censure me in your wisdom, and awake your senses... [3.2.13-17]

The same sound begins and ends each utterance: "Hear...hear", "Believe...believe", and (with some strain, not quite matching) "Censure...senses". It sounds stylish; it is also, at times, vapid, the sustaining of the style entailing a reduction in the sense. (The sentence beginning "Believe me for mine honour" seems merely tautological.) The conspicuous repetitions recur: "As Caesar loved me, I weep for him; as he was fortunate, I rejoice at it; as he was valiant, I honour him; but, as he was ambitious, I slew him." He concludes with rhetorical questions and exhortations in triplicate:

Who is here so base, that would be a bondman? If any, speak; for him have I offended. Who is here so rude, that would not be a Roman? If any, speak; for him have I offended. Who is here so vile, that will not love his country? If any, speak; for him have I offended.

It's a proficiently stylish display; it associates the conspirators with Roman freedom; and it satisfies the hearers. But the conspicuous patterning does impart some qualities of cold artifice and slick cleverness to the speech. Brutus knows all about such rhetorical figures as anaphora, parison and isocolon. In that initial "Hear me" quotation, he uses epanalepsis (the same word at the beginning and end of a statement) and polyptoton (echoing one word with another). In the "As Caesar loved me" quotation, he uses anaphora (a word repeated at the beginning of a series of statements), parison (word corresponding to word), and isocolon (statements of equal length in the passage), and he arranges the phrasing in parallel triplets with repeated endings (epistrophe).

The members of the crowd are suitably impressed, including one naive enthusiast who (with unwitting irony) cries "Let him be Caesar!", and another who (referring gauchely to crowning) says "Caesar's better parts   / Shall be crowned in Brutus". A. D. Nuttall says that the four words, "Let him be Caesar!" constitute "the most telling political moment in the history of drama": the mindless cry is laden with "the burden of a dark futurity". Far from being liberated republicans, these Romans are attuned only to autocratic rule. The people then hope to escort Brutus home; but, in a characteristic misjudgement, Brutus tells them to stay to hear Mark Antony.

Antony's verse oration beginning "Friends, Romans, countrymen, lend me your ears" is, of course, a masterpiece: Nuttall deems it "the greatest oration in the English language". The Roman orator Quintilian, in his *Institutio oratoria*, contrasts two styles: the Attic, which is refined, polished and economical, and the Asiatic, which is swelling and exultant. Whereas Brutus espoused the Attic style, Antony prefers the Asiatic.

Antony's speech opens with a lie: "I come to bury Caesar, not to praise him".   Gradually, while

114

repeating with insidiously-increasing irony (attaining sarcasm) the phrase that Brutus "is an honourable man", he reminds the hearers of Caesar's generosity to Rome and his refusal of the crown – no sign of ambition. The crowd is steadily won over. Antony then, standing by Caesar's corpse and holding the bloodstained mantle, tells how Caesar was repeatedly stabbed in an act of "bloody treason": the "honourable men" are now simply "traitors". His passionate tirade makes Brutus's oration seem tame by contrast. The people weep; and so does Antony ("good method-actor that he is", notes Nuttall): "His eyes are red as fire with weeping". And if the people are now weeping at the sight of the mantle, a grimmer spectacle is in store: in a deft move, Antony reveals the corpse itself. The butchered body silently condemns the conspirators' pretexts. Now the people demand revenge. Exploiting anti-rhetorical rhetoric, Antony, with crafty assumed modesty, says:

> I am no orator, as Brutus is,
> But (as you know me all) a plain blunt man
> That love my friend...

If, however, he says, he had the eloquence of Brutus, he would make "the very stones of Rome to rise and mutiny." Nuttall explains that Brutus exploits the figure known as "occultatio" ("concealment"), whereby information is "slipped into the hearer's mind, as it were, by the back door", as when he claims that he does not propose to read Caesar's will.

Antony's final master-stroke is to reveal to the crowd that that very will has bequeathed money to everybody and has decreed that Caesar's private gardens are now public recreation-areas. The crowd then becomes riotous, and, we are told, Brutus and Cassius flee.

Antony's oratory is thus a superb piece of calculated theatre. While apparently being swept by growing waves of emotion himself (and to a large extent he, weeping, genuinely *is* being swept), he is riding them; and he knows how to elicit the emotions of the crowd as if he were the conductor of an orchestra of enthusiastic amateurs. He also brings to mind a modern actor's cynical maxim, "Honesty, ...as soon as I can learn to fake that, I've got it made." (Later versions substitute "Sincerity" for "Honesty".) But Antony also exploits a familiar characteristic of crowds in Shakespeare's plays: they tend to be fickle in allegiance: they are thus notably manipulable, whether the manipulator be Richard III or Henry V or (in *Coriolanus*) Menenius. As Caius Martius says scornfully to the crowd in *Coriolanus*:

> Trust ye?
> With every minute you do change a mind,
> And call him noble that was now your hate. [1.1]

In various productions of *Julius Caesar*, notably Dominic Dromgoole's at the Globe Theatre in 2014, speakers for the Roman people have been located within the theatre's audience, so that the audience become unpaid extras, comprising a vast Roman crowd. It's a transformative effect, incorporating the patrons into the play, implicating us with the manipulated hearers. While adding to the scale, it augments the historical irony of the scene.

What's more, it mockingly identifies us, the audience, with what Caska had previously called "the rabblement", "the rag-tag people", and "the common herd" with "stinking breath". Those committed republicans are no democrats. Opposing Caesar-worship, Flavius and Murellus (tribunes supposedly representing the ordinary people) had praised Pompey and scorned the commoners. Indeed, *republicanism itself seems already a lost cause*, given that the commoners repeatedly seek a heroic leader: if not Caesar, then Brutus; if not Brutus, then Mark Antony.

After the noisy violence of the riot, there's a risk that the final scenes of the staged play may seem anti-climactic. Good direction should make clear that this plot is sustained by a dense meshwork of ironies which (with the audience's co-authorship) find their completion in the closing scenes, as Caesar's revenge is brought about by blunders, myopia and misinterpretation.

3. The quarrel of Brutus and Cassius: what does it prove?

It's a general rule in Shakespearian drama that characters who conspire in a murder subsequently fall to dissension. Examples are: the two murderers of the "Princes in the Tower" in *Richard III*; Richard and Buckingham in the same play; Henry IV and Exton in *Richard II*; Macbeth and Lady Macbeth; Mark Antony and Octavius in *Antony and Cleopatra*; and, famously, in *Julius Caesar*, Brutus and Cassius.

This quarrel scene (4.2) was an established theatrical success at least as early as 1640. Leonard Digges' commemorative poem about Shakespeare, published in the 1640 Folio of Shakespeare's works, says:

So have I seen, when Cesar would appeare,
And on the Stage at halfe-sword parley were,
Brutus and *Cassius*: oh how the Audience
Were ravish'd, with what wonder they went hence.

In the eighteenth century, Dr Johnson noted that this scene of the quarrel is "universally celebrated" (though he, exceptionally, found it "somewhat cold and unaffecting").

The reasons for its celebration are evident. In this scene, the natures of Brutus and Cassius are revealingly explored. The flaws and merits of both men are exposed. Their quarrel builds to a fine climax and is at last resolved in a touching display of mutual affection. Shakespeare is here at the peak of his powers as an analyst of character and as crafty playwright making the sparks fly from a passionate inter-action of two angered allies.

Initially, Brutus condemns Cassius for having "an itching palm", for being corrupt in taking bribes and defending a bribe-taker. What's more, when Brutus asked Cassius for money (Brutus declining to raise money by "base means", as Cassius evidently raises it), Cassius failed to provide it. Cassius does not refute the allegations of his own corruption; indeed, he says, "a friend should bear his friend's infirmities", thus verifying the allegations. Eventually, Cassius's response takes the form of a histrionic gesture: he offers his dagger and his bare chest so that Brutus can slay him if Brutus wishes. (Inevitably, we recall similar apparently self-sacrificing offers by Caesar and Mark Antony – and, in a different play, by the crafty Richard of Gloucester, before he becomes Richard III.) At this, Brutus's animus is at once dissipated, and he becomes forgiving. "I was ill-tempered, too", he concedes. They embrace, reconciled. Then Brutus reveals that he has learnt of the death of his wife, Portia. Cassius, astonished, comments: "How 'scaped I killing, when I crossed you so?".

The scene confirms Cassius's corruption, but reveals his genuine love for Brutus and his anguish when Brutus condemns him. Brutus, in turn, is shown to be hypocritical in his pride (he is willing to seek money which he knows Cassius has obtained illegitimately), but also sincere in his eventual wish for reconciliation. The scene as a whole is a masterpiece in its moving rendition of flawed humanity. Now it is not Brutus and Cassius but Antony and Octavius who appear the ruthless killers: the triumvirs, we are told, have ordered the deaths of at least seventy senators, including Cicero. The depiction of Brutus and Cassius may even bring to mind the words of Mariana in *Measure for Measure*:

They say best men are moulded out of faults,
And, for the most, become much more the better
For being a little bad... [5.1]

The quarrel scene confirms Shakespeare's general strategy in *Julius Caesar*: to reconcile decisive action with ambiguous characterisation. Ambivalent figures generate decisive events.

Brutus: hypocritical Stoic?

To lose a wife *once* may be regarded as a misfortune; to lose her *twice* looks like carelessness. In the Folio version of what is now Act 4, scene 2, something peculiar happens. The death of Portia is announced not once but twice; and Brutus's responses differ dramatically. Why is this?

Cassius has accused Brutus of not exemplifying his stoical philosophy, since Stoics strive to be unmoved by circumstances. Brutus responds: "No man bears sorrow better. Portia is dead." Cassius is shocked. Brutus explains the circumstances of Portia's suicide, concluding: "Speak no more of her. – Give me a bowl of wine."

That sequence spans lines 195-208. (Line numberings refer to the Watts text.) Five lines later, at 213, Titinius and Messala enter. Brutus suspects that Messala is concealing what he knows of Portia. Messala is obliged to admit: "Tis certain she is dead, and by strange manner." Brutus responds:

Why, farewell, Portia. – We must die, Messala:
By meditating that she must die once,
I have the patience to endure it now.

Duly impressed, Messala replies: "Even so great men great losses should endure."

This is very odd. The same event is announced in two different ways, and each time Brutus responds as if it were the first time. One way of explaining the second occurrence is to say that Brutus's hypocrisy is being revealed. Although he already knows that

121

Portia is dead, he pretends to Messala that he is learning the news for the first time, so that he can make a practised stoical reply, thus impressing Messala.

Another way of explaining the repetition, and one favoured by numerous editors, is to speculate as follows. Perhaps Shakespeare, after writing one version, changed his mind and wrote another; but although one was supposed to be cancelled, in the Folio it remained in print alongside the other. But then editors have to decide *which* of the two Shakespeare meant to cancel: lines 193-208 or 231-245. Curiously, *both* look like later insertions into the scene.

So, if you are staging the play, you find that you have at least four options here. 1: You keep both the passages. Then the audience sees unexpected deviousness from Brutus: he seems cunningly manipulative. 2: Cut lines 231-245 (the Messala entry), thus accentuating the relatively gentle Brutus and his reconciliation with the now-sympathetic Cassius. 3: Cut lines 193-208, to show Brutus as toughly stoical. 4: Delete both the disputed passages. This way you don't solve the problem; you dissolve it.

In my edition of the text, I chose the first option. Thus I was true to the First Folio. If I were staging the play, however, I would adopt the option which seems to be the most consistent with the broad context. I think that passage 231-245 depicts Brutus as too severe, and that the earlier passage represents Shakespeare's improvement, true to the relatively mild character of Brutus and the intensity of Portia's devotion. So I would adopt option 2 and cut lines 231-245.

This puzzle demonstrates what literary critics are generally reluctant to concede: for Shakespearian material, different solutions are appropriate in different contexts. An editor has a duty to make clear the nature of the crux, so that readers may assess the alternatives. A director of the play, in contrast, has a duty to coordinate the textual material in the light of his or her interpretation. In that case, the democratic choices for the spectators are generated by their awareness of the "mutual jars" – the discrepancies – between different productions. Either way, the multiplicity of *Julius Caesar* should thrive.

"Crowds are a problem."

Professor Alan Sinfield, a "Cultural Materialist" (i.e., a critic indebted to Karl Marx and Raymond Williams), has said that in Shakespeare's plays,

crowds are a problem. You can't present the crowd in Shakespeare's Rome as if they were the modern, organised industrial working class... The fickleness of this mob... is a real characteristic of a pre-industrial city crowd, united only temporarily to riot over a specific grievance...

What the director *can* do is present the crowd with respect, as people driven to desperation by poverty and extortion.

In *Julius Caesar*, however, the mob that murders Cinna the poet clearly does not deserve "respect", and there is no evidence that those rioters are driven by "poverty and extortion"; on the contrary, they have been enflamed by Antony's rhetoric which has emphasised Caesar's generosity in leaving so much money and land to the people. Act 3, sc. 2, superbly orchestrates the way in which the plebeians, responding hastily and eagerly to the orators, change from approving the conspirators to seeking to destroy them (and parts of the city too), urging each other on to a crescendo of passionate destructiveness ending with the mindless "anything!":

> PLEB. 1:　　...Come, away, away!
> 　　　　　We'll burn his body in the holy place,
> 　　　　　And with the brands fire the traitors'
> 　　　　　　　　　　　　　　　houses.
> 　　　　　Take up the body.

PLEB. 4: Go fetch fire.
PLEB. 3: Pluck down benches.
PLEB. 5: Pluck down forms, windows, anything!

This crowd brings to mind Marx's *"Lumpenproletariat"* ("rabble"), defined by him in *The Manifesto of the Communist Party* as "the 'dangerous class', the social scum": "its conditions of life... prepare it... for the part of a bribed tool of reactionary intrigue". The phrase "social scum" seems excessive, and the first plebeian is even granted the brief accolade of two lines of iambic pentameter; but the Roman mob has indeed been bribed and is certainly the "tool of reactionary intrigue". (Even the witty cobbler of Act 1, sc. 1, was an admirer of Caesar, and may have become part of this crowd.) Perhaps Marx, who so greatly admired *Timon of Athens*, has in this part of the *Manifesto* been influenced by *Julius Caesar.*

Why is misinterpretation important?

Julius Caesar abounds in interwoven themes. These include: public versus private commitments; the political versus the familial; the secular beset by the supernatural; power that may corrupt; noble ideals subverted by harsh action and fallible agents; the powers and perils of rhetoric; free will confronting augury, chance, and perhaps destiny; and, of course, "the return of the repressed". Related to the last item is the theme of misinterpretation.

After Cassius commits suicide, Titinius enters, bearing a "wreath of victory" from Brutus to present to the dead leader. Understanding Cassius's fatal error, Titinius cries: "Alas, thou hast miscónstrued everything!". Marjorie Garber, in her study entitled *Dream in Shakespeare*, says that this cry might serve as an epigraph for the whole play:

The play is full of omens and portents, augury and dreams, and almost without exception these omens are misinterpreted. Calpurnia's dream, the dream of Cinna the poet, the advice of the augurers, all suggest one course of action and produce its opposite.

As Cicero observes,

> Indeed, it is a strange-disposèd time;
> But men may cónstrue things after their fashion,
> Clean from the purpose of the things themselves.
>
> [1.3]

Decius deliberately misinterprets Calphurnia's dream of the statue spouting blood, in order to persuade Caesar to go to the Capitol. To see it as a warning not to go is wrong, Decius says; "This dream is all amiss interpreted". It shows, he claims, that

> from you great Rome shall suck
> Reviving blood, and that great men shall press
> For tinctures, stains, reliques, and cognizance.
> [2.2]

Symbolically, says Garber, this foreshadows events to come. "Decius, who means to assert control, is in a larger sense controlled, since he does not see that his interpretation is true." Again, malicious misconstruing occurs when the plebeians take the name for the man, murdering the poet merely for bearing the name "Cinna".

Garber concludes:

Julius Caesar...does not concern itself principally with political theory but rather with the strange blindness of the rational mind – in politics and elsewhere – to the great irrational powers which flow through life and control it.

At first that sounds persuasive, and her argument neatly complements the thesis of "the return of the repressed" which our account has offered. We recall not only the mob, so readily aroused to destructive passion, but also the supernatural visitations, those weird images of violent and unnatural disruption. But is Octavius, for instance, subject to the "control" of irrational powers? Doesn't he seem all too coldly rational? Again we need to recognise a grand paradox of the play: the rationality which characterises Roman discourse is powerfully beleaguered: as in the case of the mob aroused by Antony's rhetoric, there is a provocative relationship (sometimes mutually provocative) between the rationality and the contrasting insurgent irrationality.

Character and destiny

In one of the most memorable speeches of the play, Cassius declares:

> Men, at some time, are masters of their fates.
> The fault, dear Brutus, is not in our stars,
> But in ourselves, that we are underlings. [1.2]

It's a call to action, stressing the autonomy of individuals and their freedom to decide their futures. The qualification "at some time" is important: the autonomy and the freedom have temporal limits. In *Julius Caesar*, furthermore, however, that call to action is beset by ironies.

In the first place, the Roman ethos, with its emphasis on personal pride, public service, honourable duty, and "death before dishonour", has a potent effect on individuals, as Cassius's own death will show. The play suggests the large extent to which, in a given society, people are governed by value-systems which are contingent and not ubiquitous. Individuals are largely "authored" by authority: the authority of the state's traditions and values. Again, the autonomy of the self may seem to be eclipsed by sheer bad luck. Cassius's death is a consequence of a misreading of the situation. Cinna the poet dies because he has an unlucky name. And consider the opening of Act 4, sc. 1:

> ANTONY: These many then shall die; their
> names are pricked.

> OCTAVIUS [to Lepidus]: Your brother too must
> die; consent you, Lepidus?
> LEPIDUS: I do consent –
> OCTAVIUS: Prick him down, Antony, –
> LEPIDUS: Upon condition Publius shall not live,
> Who is your sister's son, Mark
> Antony.
> ANTONY: He shall not live; look, with a spot I
> damn him.

"With a spot I damn him": a spot of ink curtails a life. Rapid deaths result from a change in political fortune and from the ruthlessness of those who currently hold power. Familial loyalties are ostentatiously nullified.

This is a world in which omens are bizarrely conspicuous (e.g. a lion at the Capitol, an owl hooting at noon) but difficult to interpret. Katharine Maus comments:

> By emphasizing the analogies among personal, political, and natural forms of disruption, omens on the one hand intensify the significance of the play's characters: their decision, quirks, and flaws affect the structure of the universe itself. On the other hand, the reliability of omens challenges the notion that history is the product of personal effort, since augury implies restrictions on free will, suggesting that individuals are caught in the toils of a historical process they cannot control or understand.

The omens suggest that sometimes "the fault" *is* "in our stars", unless we take the view that the omens (however fearsome) do not *compel* but simply register and comment supernaturally upon the consequences of the operation of free will by individuals. Generally, indeed, they *do* seem to be a response to men's actions rather than the prompter of actions: thus the strange apparitions reported in Act 1, sc. 3, appear to have been occasioned by the burgeoning conspiracy against Caesar. Of course, the supernatural manifestations are so bizarre and diverse that, as is often the case with symbolic events, there remains a residue of the inexplicable.

Free will is always constrained: it operates within limits. At certain times, an opportunity occurs for an important exertion of free will, as when Brutus can choose to join or avoid the conspiracy.

"Destiny" is an imposing name given to a seemingly-inevitable sequence of events affecting perhaps a nation, a group or an individual. Nineteenth-century imperialists could assert that it was England's destiny to rule an empire. The term often implies supernatural ordinance. Destiny may be regarded as supporting or opposing the choices of free will.

In *Julius Caesar*, the plotting by people is subordinated to, and mocked by, the more potent plotting by the spirit of irony: a mischievous and less mystical version of destiny. The freely-willed intentions are so often thwarted. The conspirators seek to avert the danger of autocracy and to give their country liberty, but their actions will inaugurate a long era of autocratic rule. Again: they think they are killing Caesar, but Ceasar lives on as influential ghost: supernatural agency mocks their plans. Antony persuades Octavius that Lepidus must be cast aside (though Octavius knows Lepidus to be "a tried and valiant soldier"), but eventually, in *Antony and Cleopatra*, Antony will be defeated by his current ally, Octavius, and that conflict is portended by details in *Julius Caesar* (e.g. at 5.1.1-20).

Sometimes, then, *Julius Caesar* may bring to mind the words of Friedrich Engels, in a famous letter of 1890:

History is made in such a way that the final result always arises from conflicts between many individual wills, of which each again has been made what it is by a host of particular conditions of life. Thus there are innumerable intersecting forces, an infinite series of parallelograms of forces which give rise to one resultant – the historical event. This again may itself be viewed as the product of a power which works as a whole *unconsciously* and without volition. For what each individual wills is obstructed by everyone else, and what emerges is something that no one willed.

Engels may have been recalling Adam Smith's claim, in *The Wealth of Nations*, that human industry and folly could bring about a revolution which nobody had foreseen. *Julius Caesar* may also at times evoke the words of Joseph Conrad, who, in *Nostromo* (1904), declared that the future of a country was

being settled not so much by the industry as by the fears, necessities and crimes of men short-sighted in good and evil.

In *Julius Caesar*, Shakespeare, while giving instances of "men short-sighted in good and evil", is himself not short-sighted at all: on the contrary, he exploits bi-focal vision. Individuals loom large: we experience intimately their worries, fears, ambitions and affections. Yet, from the first scene, with its reminder that the glorious Pompey seems soon forgotten, we are also given hints of a longer time-

132

scale which may eventually become a vast perspective (revealing "states unborn and accents yet unknown") in which individuals shrink to ephemeral agents in a long historical process which nobody adequately foresees or comprehends.

In *Henry IV, Part 2*, the ageing, ailing King Henry says:

> O God, that one might read the book of Fate,
> And see the revolution of the times
> Make mountains level, and the continent,
> Weary of solid firmness, melt itself
> Into the sea;...
>   how chance's mocks
> And changes fill the cup of alteration
> With divers liquors. O, if this were seen,
> The happiest youth, viewing his progress through,
> What perils past, what crosses to ensue,
> Would shut the book, and sit him down and die.
>   [3.1]

Intermittently, *Julius Caesar* may bring such a bleak vista to mind. But that is not the dominant impression the play gives. The actions of the drama culminate in climax and closure. The closure is, in the main, morally satisfying: the conspirators who meted out murder have been defeated and have perished, after perceiving the pattern of justice, but receive generous obsequies. The multiple ironies of the action have reached their culmination, and those ironies have a powerful moral tenor. Hubris has met nemesis. Peripeteia has been identified in anagnorisis. Manipulators have been manipulated. Ambitions have been confounded. The moral structures, however, incorporate the immoral and amoral. The action of the conspirators provokes the vengeful reaction of the mob and the triumvirate, but that reaction entails the immoral (e.g. the slaying of Cinna) or a mixture of the moral and the immoral (e.g. the death-list which may punish the guilty, but which, in its brisk and casual callousness, seems excessive and is ostentatiously unfamilial).

Repeatedly in *Juilius Caesar*, a meshwork of irony is clearly conspicuous; and sustained irony implies, if not the presence of a cosmic ironist, at least the permeation of events by what may be termed a morally-attuned pattern-making force. Large-scale dramatic irony occurs when events produce a result quite different from what had been expected. Thus, assassination of a supposed autocrat results in the establishment of a corrupt triumvirate and eventually of a powerful autocracy: the opposite to what was intended. Thematic irony can occur when an utterance has a significance contrasting with what was intended: thus the plebeian who, approving Brutus, cries "Let him be Caesar!" (in Act 3, sc. 2), is endorsing the very governance that Brutus had sought to destroy.

The accumulation of manifestations of irony may seem to imply a form of destiny: notably, the operation of morally-attuned pattern-making which repeatedly serves to expose human limitations and the large capacity for error by human agents. The greater the irony, the less the sense that men are "masters of their fates". The operations of a person's free will are, we learn, historically and ideologically circumscribed, and are sapped by the competing and conflicting freely-willed choices of other people and by the inexhaustible human capacity for error. The ironies resemble grim jokes at the expense of human pride. The master-plot of *Julius Caesar* consists of *the sustained series of ambushes, large and small, with which irony besets human endeavours.* All the characters, from Julius himself to the manipulated mob, are humiliated by the morally-impelled ironist, an invisible but ubiquitous sombre jester. Octavius may seem the most clear-sighted (and he will eventually triumph); but he is tainted by corruption, he is ruthless, and, in *Antony and Cleopatra*, his success clearly requires the suppression, or absence from his nature, of warm responsive humanity. The ironist says "Here is a politically successful man: but who would wish to be him?".

People make history, but it is usually not the history they intended to make. Seeking freedom and power, they unwittingly help to knit the nets of irony in which people become enmeshed – sometimes absurdly, sometimes fatally.

It is this lesson, with its sombre wisdom, which *Julius Caesar* so intelligently (and, in the theatre, so vividly) dramatises.

How feminist is *Julius Caesar*?

Coppélia Kahn says that

the sexual difference that really counts in *Julius Caesar* isn't framed simply as one between male and female and doesn't depend on the presence or absence of female characters.

The ideology of the Roman republic, she explains, depended on the distinction between (i) politics as the freely willed action of rational men and (ii) the household as the realm of mere physical necessity, of women, children and slaves. In the play, "as long as Brutus sees himself in another man's eyes, he is a Roman, whole and coherent"; but when Portia in Act 2, sc. 1, reflects an image of him as divided and troubled , that Roman identity is compromised.

As for Caesar, Kahn argues that though he depicts himself as constant and unwavering,

his constancy, like his refusal of the crown, seems transparently an act, a pretense at being the firm Roman, belied by his "feminine" mutability and identification with maternal rather than masculine styles of power.

Furthermore, the assassination itself "resoundingly feminizes Caesar": his punctured body makes men cry, and Antony likens the wounds to eyes weeping or dumb mouths that beg an orator to speak for them. The ensuing revenge, Kahn claims, has a feminine character: pity and tears are transmuted into fury and strife, "reminiscent of the Furies or the crazed female worshippers of Dionysus". Thus:

When Caesar...has been feminized and brought low, the most fearsome and destructive images of the feminine possess Rome. Again, one might say, the repressed returns.

Here one might object that Kahn is pressing her case too far and is invoking and endorsing demeaning stereotypes of the female. As we have seen, the most striking illustration of the insensate violence of the mob is the destruction of the innocent poet, Cinna. Here we see a man torn by men (the text specifies that they are male: "Answer every man directly"); so that allusions to the Furies or the Bacchantes seem inappropriate. If, however, it be argued that insensate violence, being irrational, is necessarily feminine in character, this would seem to reinstate a misogynistic stereotyping of women as irrational; and this would be inappropriate to a text in which Calphurnia and Portia are seen to reason so cogently with their menfolk. Yet, for all her cogency, Portia still makes familiar demeaning concessions:

> I have a man's mind, but a woman's might.
> How hard it is for women to keep counsel!...
> > Ay me, how weak a thing
> The heart of woman is! [2.4]

Portia shows Brutus (who had referred to "the melting spirits of women") the self-inflicted wound in her thigh. Coppélia Kahn asserts that the wound "destabilizes the gendered concept of virtue". Portia seeks to express the masculine ideal of constancy, but she also evokes femininity (the bleeding wound in the thigh hinting at "a genital wound" and "the capacity to be penetrated"). The wound is "ambiguously, undecidably feminine *and* masculine": thus, "the constitution of manly virtue requires the repression of the feminine, and the repressed returns".

But what of her eventual death, when she "swallowed fire"? Alas, here repression prevails: "Shakespeare abandons his earlier ambiguity and reinscribes sexual difference". Kahn, associating irrationality with the feminine, declares:

Her crazed, bizarre act of self-destruction reinserts her firmly into the feminine, while Brutus's suicide signifies his *virtus* [manly virtue].

On the other hand, we may be inclined to argue that though her method of suicide is bizarre, Portia is motivated by concern for her husband. She grieves for his absence, and is alarmed by the headway of Mark Antony and Octavius against him. In contrast, the suicide of Brutus (who had reproved Cato for committing suicide) is tellingly and almost embarrassingly self-centred:

I shall have glory by this losing day,
More than Octavius and Mark Antony
By this vile conquest shall attain unto... [5.5]

Indeed, to these words, one response that comes to mind is, again, Mercutio's in *Romeo and Juliet*: "A plague o' both your houses!".

Another commentator, Katharine Maus, emphasises the impotence of the women in the play. She says that the "feminine intuition" of Calphurnia and Portia has no practical effect.

Nobility for these radically marginalized characters requires them to internalize values that for them have little use.

Portia's self-wounding, according to Maus, is "a gesture that suggests a self-castration, as if a woman were at best a slashed man", while Portia's death (in which she seeks to imitate masculine fortitude) "seems pointlessly masochistic". Arguably, we may again respond, both actions have a point: an expression, however desperate, of love and concern.

Roman culture marginalises the women, and Cassius defines the "womanish" as weak and submissive; but Shakespeare makes clear the cost of that marginalisation. The price is paid by men, too.

To the extent that the marginalisation of women is a subordination or denial of the familial, it entails neglect of a paradigm of sociable politics: the possibility of a society which is "familial" in cherishing constructive co-operation, mutual support and sustenance. The politics that dominate Rome are masculine, emulous, competitive, and, all too often, destructive.

Chapter 5: The play's political influence

What is *Julius Caesar's* political legacy?

The historic legacy of *Julius Caesar* includes not only murder and perhaps mass slaughter but also hope and reconciliation.

1. *Julius Caesar* and the assassination of President Lincoln

John Wilkes Booth, a famed and successful actor, assassinated President Abraham Lincoln at Ford's Theatre in Washington D.C. on April 14th, 1865.

The father of John Wilkes Booth was Junius Brutus Booth, an eminent British actor whose first names derived from the Brutus commemorated in *Julius Caesar*. The forename "Wilkes" honours John Wilkes, the British radical journalist and politician who had supported the American rebels during the American War of Independence. John Wilkes Booth was a confederate sympathiser who opposed the abolition of slavery.

According to one eye-witness, J. W. Booth, having shot Lincoln in the head, leapt down from the President's box to the stage, and shouted "*Sic semper tyrannis!*" (Latin for "Thus always to tyrants!") before fleeing. Booth himself claimed that he shouted "*Sic semper!*" before firing his pistol at the President. The Latin exclamation "*Sic semper tyrannis!*" had been attributed to the historic Brutus at Caesar's assassination, but it probably derived from a declaration ascribed by the historian Thucydides to the rebellious Alcibiades, who declared "*semper enim tyrannis fuimus infesti*": "for we have always been dangerous to tyrants". Adapted, it became the motto of the Commonwealth of Virginia.

Booth had played the parts of Brutus and Mark Antony; he said that his favourite character was Brutus. He accused Lincoln of "making himself a king", the very accusation made against Caesar by his assassins. Shortly before being ambushed and shot, Booth wrote in his diary: "With every man's hand against me, I am here in despair. And why[?] For doing what Brutus was honored for, what made Tell a hero. And yet I for striking down a greater tyrant than they ever knew am looked upon as a common cutthroat."

Thus Shakespeare's Brutus, perceived as a foe of tyranny, helped to prompt the assassination of an American President.

On 19 April 1995, a terrorist bomb-attack in Oklahoma City killed 168 people and destroyed many buildings. Timothy McVeigh, who would be sentenced to death for his leading role in the attack, was arrested on the same day as the atrocity. He was wearing a tee-shirt bearing that ominous phrase "*sic semper tyrannis*" and a picture of Lincoln. Thus violence generates violence. Brutus had a long legacy.

2. Nelson Mandela and *Julius Caesar*

As a young man, Nelson Mandela worked to establish the Youth League of the African National Congress. The League's manifesto ended with an exhortation to action: Cassius's words, "The fault, dear Brutus, lies not in our stars, / But in ourselves, that we are underlings." Mandela later remarked, "Somehow, Shakespeare always seems to have something to say to us."

When Mandela was imprisoned on Robben Island, the prisoners passed round "the Robben Island Bible". This was the Peter Alexander edition of Shakespeare's *Complete Works*, smuggled in, its covers disguised with Hindu images. Mandela selected as his favourite passage some lines from *Julius Caesar*. He marked them with vertical strokes in the margin and the dated signature "N. R. D. Mandela 16.12.77" alongside it. The passage, which he evidently found sustaining, was this:

> Cowards die many times before their deaths:
> The valiant never taste of death but once.
> Of all the wonders that I yet have heard,
> It seems to me most strange that men should fear,
> Seeing that death, a necessary end,
> Will come when it will come.
> > [2.2.32-7: Alexander text.]

Thus the proud words that Shakespeare attributed to Julius Caesar helped to sustain Nelson Mandela, who, after serving 27 years in jail for "conspiracy to overthrow the state", emerged to become President of South Africa (1994-99) and a greatly admired statesman. Mandela, who advocated the reconciliation of former foes, would have known that Caesar had sometimes forgiven and even promoted his former enemies. 16 December, the day and month of the inscription, would become South Africa's Reconciliation Day.

What makes the play so fully political?

In *Caesar: The Life of a Colossus*, the historian
Adrian Goldsworthy says this of the real-life
conspiracy against Caesar:

> The conspirators spoke of liberty, and believed that this
> could only be restored by removing Caesar. Most, perhaps
> all, felt that they were acting for the good of the entire
> Republic... Liberty and the cry of a return to the Republic
> also meant a return to the dominance of a few well-
> established families, and the opportunity to bribe the
> electorate and make fortunes by exploiting the inhabitants
> of the provinces...
> Caesar was a rational man and judged that Rome needed
> him, because without him it would simply relapse into civil
> war. He was dictator and he was effectively a monarch, but
> he was not a cruel one and used his powers for the general
> good... [Caesar] throughout his career had consistently
> advocated measures for the benefit of the wider population
> and not simply the narrow elite...

Goldsworthy's comments may remind us that
Julius Caesar, while depicting Caesar's vanity and
fallibility and Brutus's nobility, notes the corrupt
practices of Cassius, Mark Antony, Octavius and
Lepidus, and cites the public gifts made by Caesar in
his will. The conspirators are eventually punished.
The comments also remind us that *Julius Caesar* is a
masterpiece of searching ambivalence, so that Caesar,
persuasively depicted as noble benefactor by Mark
Antony, can be linked, in performances, to Fascist

dictators. The splendours of the Roman empire, after all, were facilitated largely by robbery with violence.

Geoffrey Bullough says that in *Julius Caesar*, Shakespeare achieves

a somewhat detached tolerance in his attitude towards historical figures, and at the same time a critical attitude towards politics and those who take part in it... But the mood is still benevolent and the ancient world has a certain grandeur.

"Benevolent"? Perhaps "stoical" would be an apter adjective. The "certain grandeur" is amply evident in the depiction of Rome and Roman values; but both are subject to subversive pressures. That "critical attitude" is intelligently resourceful and ironigenic – it breeds ironies. The "grandeur" derives partly from the proudly self-aware stances of the protagonists, and largely from the eloquent rhetoric, some of which warns us to beware of eloquent rhetoric in the political world.

In fact, what makes the play so *fully* political is that Shakespeare sees *beyond* the political. While transmuting historical events into poetry of memorable eloquence, distilling reported strife into auditory beauty, and converting legendary violence into interrogatory entertainment, he shows the high price in human terms that may be exacted by political commitments. In Shakespeare's world, political ambitions even tend to become unnatural, to the extent that they become anti-familial: this is demonstrated not only by *Julius Caesar* but also by *Hamlet, Macbeth* and *King Lear*. Shakespeare shows that, all too often, political rhetoric veils private realities and may facilitate human suffering; human endeavours prove counter-productive; real outcomes exceed and mock the outcomes that were intended; and the ambitions of a few people cost the lives of many.

Therefore, in view of the turmoil and carnage currently besetting much of the world, *Julius Caesar* is as timely as ever.

Bibliography

Barthes, Roland: "La mort de l'auteur" [1968], rendered as "The Death of the Author" in Barthes's *Image Music Text*, translated by Stephen Heath (New York: Hill and Wang, 1977).

Bayley, John: *Shakespeare and Tragedy.* London: Routledge & Kegan Paul, 1981.

Bloom, Harold: *Shakespeare: The Invention of the Human.* New York: Riverhead Books, 1998.

Bradbook, M. C.: *Shakespeare the Craftsman: The Clark Lectures.* London: Chatto & Windus, 1969.

Bullough, Geoffrey, ed.: *Narrative and Dramatic Sources of Shakespeare: Vol. 5: The Roman Plays.* London: Routledge & Kegan Paul, 1964.

Burrow, Colin: "Very New and Very Old" in *Around the Globe*, Issue 57 (Summer 2014), pp.24-5.

Carlier, J. C.: "Roland Barthes's Resurrection of the Author and Redemption of Biography": Item 49 of *Roland Barthes*, ed. Mike and Nicholas Gane (London: Sage, 2004), Vol. 3.

Conrad, Joseph: *Nostromo* [1904 text], ed. Cedric Watts. London: Dent Everyman Orion, 1995.

Cookson, Linda, and Loughrey, Bryan, ed.: *Longman Critical Essays: "Julius Caesar"*. Harlow: Longman, 1992.

Daiches, David: *Literary Essays*. Chicago: Chicago U. P., 1956.
Daiches, David: *Shakespeare: "Julius Caesar"*. London: Arnold, 1976.

Dean, Leonard F., ed.: *Twentieth Century Interpretations of "Julius Caesar"*. Englewood Cliffs, N.J.: Prentice-Hall, 1968.

Dryden, John: "Prologue" to *Aurung-Zebe* [1676]. *The Works of John Dryden*, Vol. XII, ed. Vinton A. Dearing. London: University of California Press, 1994.

Elloway, David: *Julius Caesar*. Basingstoke: Macmillan, 1986.

Engels, Friedrich: letter to J. Bloch, 21.9.1890. See: www.marxists.org/archive/marx/works/letters/90.

Garber, Marjorie: *Dream in Shakespeare: From Metaphor to Metamorphosis*. New Haven and London: Yale U. P., 2013.

Gielgud, Sir John: "Foreword" to John F. Andrews, ed.: William Shakespeare: *Julius Caesar*. London: Everyman / Dent / Orion, 1993.

Goldsworthy, Adrian: *Caesar: The Life of a Colossus* [2006]. London: Phoenix, 2007.

Hadfield, Andrew: *Shakespeare and Renaissance Politics*. London: Thomson Learning, 2004.

Hamer, Mary: *William Shakespeare: "Julius Caesar"*. Plymouth: Northcote House, 1998.

Hazlitt, William: *Characters of Shakespear's Plays* [1817]. London: Dent, no date.

Holden, Anthony: *William Shakespeare: His Life and Work* [1999]. London: Abacus, 2000.

Holderness, Graham, Loughrey, Bryan, and Murphy, Andrew, ed.: *Shakespeare: The Roman Plays*. Harlow: Longman, 1996.

Humphreys, Arthur: "Introduction" to Humphreys, ed.: William Shakespeare: *Julius Caesar*. Oxford: Oxford U. P., 1984.

Jonson, Ben: "To the Memory of my Beloved, the Author, Mr. William Shakespeare: and what he hath left us" in *Poems of Ben Jonson*, ed. G B. Johnston. London: Routledge & Kegan Paul, 1954.
Jonson, Ben: *Discoveries* [1641]. Edinburgh: Edinburgh U. P., 1966.

Kahn, Coppélia: *Roman Shakespeare: Warriors, Wounds and Women*. London: Routledge, 1997.

Kastan, David Scott, ed.: *A Companion to Shakespeare*. Oxford: Blackwell, 1999.

Kauffman, Michael W: *American Brutus: John Wilkes Booth and the Lincoln Conspiracies.* New York: Random House, 2004.

Kermode, Frank: *Shakespeare's Language* [2000]. London: Penguin, 2001.

Knight, G. Wilson: *The Imperial Theme* [1931]. London: Methuen, 1961.

Knights, L. C.: "Shakespeare and Political Wisdom" in *Twentieth Century Interpretations of "Julius Caesar"*, ed. Leonard F. Dean. Englewood Cliffs, N. J.: Prentice-Hall, 1968.

Maus, Katharine Eisaman: introduction to *Julius Caesar* in *The Norton Shakespeare*, ed. Stephen Greenblatt *et al.* New York and London: Norton, 1997.

Maxwell, J. C.: "Shakespeare: The Middle Plays" in *The Age of Shakespeare*, ed. Boris Ford. Harmondsworth: Penguin, 1955.

Miles, Geoffrey: *Shakespeare and the Constant Romans.* Oxford: Oxford U. P., 1996.

Miola, Robert S.: "*Julius Caesar* and the Tyrannicide Debate": *Renaissance Quarterly* 38 (Summer 1985), 271-89.
Miola, Robert S.: *Shakespeare's Rome.* Cambridge: Cambridge U. P., 1983.

Miola, Robert S.: "Reading the Classics" in D. S. Kastan, ed.: *A Companion to Shakespeare*. Oxford: Blackwell, 1999.

Nuttall, A. D.: *A New Mimesis*. London and New York: Methuen, 1983.
Nuttall, A. D.: *Shakespeare the Thinker*. New Haven and London: Yale U. P., 2007.

Poole, Adrian: *The Connell Guide to Shakespeare's 'Antony and Cleopatra'*. Chippenham: Connell Guides, 2012.

Ripley, John: *"Julius Caesar" on Stage in England and America 1599-1973*. Cambridge: Cambridge U. P., 1980.

Schanzer, Ernest: "Thomas Platter's Observations on the Elizabethan Stage": *Notes and Queries* 201 (1956), 465-7.
Schanzer, Ernest: *The Problem Plays of Shakespeare*. London: Routledge & Kegan Paul, 1963.

Shaw, George Bernard: review (1898) of Beerbohm Tree's production of *Julius Caesar*. See *Shaw on Shakespeare*, ed. Edwin Wilson. London: Cassell, 1962.

Smith, Adam: *The Wealth of Nations*. London: Dent, 1910.

Spurgeon, Caroline F. E.: *Shakespeare's Imagery and What It Tells Us* [1935]. Cambridge: Cambridge U. P., 1965.

Sutherland, John, and Watts, Cedric: *Henry V, War Criminal? and Other Shakespeare Puzzles*. Oxford: Oxford U. P., 2000.

Thomas, Vivian: *"Julius Caesar"*. Hemel Hempstead: Harvester Wheatsheaf, 1992.

Traversi, D. A.: *Shakespeare: The Roman Plays*. London: Hollis & Carter, 1963.

Ure, Peter, ed.: *"Julius Caesar": A Casebook*. London: Macmillan, 1969.

Van Doren, Mark: *Shakespeare*. London: Allen and Unwin, 1941.

Watts, Cedric: *Final Exam: A Novel* (by "Peter Green"). London: PublishNation, 2013.
Watts, Cedric: *Shakespeare Puzzles*. London: PublishNation, 2014.
Watts, Cedric: *The Connell Guide to Shakespeare's Second Tetralogy*. London: Connell Guides, 2014.

Weever, John: *The Mirror of Martyrs*: quoted in *Shakespeare and His Critics*, ed. F. E. Halliday. London: Duckworth, 1958.

Wilson, Richard: *Will Power: Essays on Shakespearean Authority*. Brighton: Harvester Wheatsheaf, 1993.
Wilson, Richard, ed.: *New Casebooks: "Julius Caesar": William Shakespeare*. Basingstoke: Palgrave, 2002.

www.ingramcontent.com/pod-product-compliance
Lightning Source LLC
Chambersburg PA
CBHW060519290526

45791CB00001B/448